Black Theology— Essays on Gender Perspectives

Black Theology— Essays on Gender Perspectives

Dwight N. Hopkins

CASCADE Books • Eugene, Oregon

BLACK THEOLOGY—ESSAYS ON GENDER PERSPECTIVES

Copyright © 2017 Dwight N. Hopkins. All rights reserved. Except for brief quotations in critical publications or reviews, no part of this book may be reproduced in any manner without prior written permission from the publisher. Write: Permissions, Wipf and Stock Publishers, 199 W. 8th Ave., Suite 3, Eugene, OR 97401.

Cascade Books
An Imprint of Wipf and Stock Publishers
199 W. 8th Ave., Suite 3
Eugene, OR 97401

www.wipfandstock.com

PAPERBACK ISBN: 978-1-5326-0818-6
HARDCOVER ISBN: 978-1-5326-0820-9
EBOOK ISBN: 978-1-5326-0819-3

Cataloguing-in-Publication data:

Names: Hopkins, Dwight N., author.

Title: Black theology—essays on gender perspectives / Dwight N. Hopkins.

Description: Eugene, OR: Cascade Books, 2017.

Identifiers: ISBN 978-1-5326-0818-6 (paperback) | ISBN 978-1-5326-0820-9 (hardcover) | ISBN 978-1-5326-0819-3 (ebook)

Subjects: LCSH: Black theology | Liberation theology.

Classification: BT82.7 H661 2017 (print) | BT82.7 (ebook).

Manufactured in the U.S.A.   06/22/17

For my

Father, Robert R. Hopkins, Sr.
Grandfathers, William and Charles
Great Grandfathers, John and Stephen

Contents

Introduction | ix

Part 1: The Black Man and Gender Studies

1. Two Black Male Leaders: Barack Obama and Jeremiah Wright (2008) | 3
2. A New Black Heterosexual Male (2001) | 23
3. Poor Brother, Rich Brother: Faith, Family, and Education (1991) | 33
4. The Construction of the Black Male Body: Eroticism and Religion (2004) | 39
5. L.A. and the City: What's God Got to Do with It? (1994) | 57

Part 2: The Black Man and Black Women

6. Black Theology of Liberation and the Impact of Womanist Theology (2002) | 75
7. Womanist Gardens and Lies above Suspicion (2006) | 89
8. Enslaved Black Women: A Theology of Justice and Reparations (2010) | 98
9. Black Women's Spirituality of Funk (1993) | 118
10. Working Together: Black and Womanist Theologies (2010) | 144

Introduction

I am the son of Robert R. Hopkins Sr., the grandson of William and Charles, and the great-grandson of John and Stephen. We all come from Virginia. My father's father (William) owned three businesses: one each in transportation, energy, and food processing. In addition, he owned over forty acres of land. Similarly, my father's grandfather (John) owned land.

My mother's father (Charles) owned his business as a commercial tobacco farmer and sold tobacco on the open market. He also owned a family farm where his family lived and where he grew all the fruits, vegetables, and farm animals needed to take care of his wife, children, and grandchildren. My father preferred to leave the countryside and with his wife raise his family in the city of Richmond. After buying a house for them, there he became an unsupervised skilled worker for the Chesapeake and Ohio Railroad Company. Later in life, I learned from family members how momentous an achievement it was for a Colored man to be unsupervised and possess a skill during the postslavery-culture of Virginia, with its legal segregation and strict racial customs of dos and don'ts.

The first memories I have of my tobacco-farmer grandfather (Charles) comes from the yearly summer months I used to spend on his family farm along with his other grandsons. We each had our daily duties. Mine consisted of walking the mule to the creek and rising very early in the morning to go with my grandmother to the chicken coop to get eggs. Papa (as we called him) was a tall black, African man. In fact, the family oral tradition places him in the Akan ethnic group of Ghana. I look like him and have been mistaken for an Akan in Ghana and by the many Ghanaians I have met in the United States and on my travels throughout the world. Likewise, my friends from other African countries routinely assume I have an Akan family tree. Thus my Ghanaian and additional African friends and acquaintances, along with global unplanned meetings with others from that country, corroborate this family African connection.

Papa stood tall, especially to a grandson who grew up around him during the summers. From my ages five to eight, he made a permanent impression on me. He stood as a mountain, the one always physically present for his wife, children, and grandchildren. Papa managed both the business farm and the family-sustenance farm. He seemed to be able to build and fix anything: his house, the barn, the wagons pulled by the mules, and more. And he read his Bible and attended church. My mountain grandfather was a solid family fixture and lived each day based on duty—duty to his wife, duty to his children, and duty to his grandchildren.

In fact my father shared this same practice of duty. For instance, another fond memory of summer on Papa's farm is sitting in the backseat of my father's car while he drove Papa on errands. My father was Papa's son-in-law, and the duty of a son-in-law is to respect his father-in-law and serve his elder. Because Papa was the father of my father's wife, my father took his duty commitments very seriously. In that car rode three generations. That remains one of my most memorable, beautiful moments as a very young boy.

And like his father and father-in-law, my father carried on the role of mountain. In fact, he remained present until he died at ninety-five years. His children always knew where he was, mainly at work or home during the weekdays, or weekend family trips or hunting and fishing, or serving as an usher at Sunday church. For most of the times, he stayed at home to open the door for his children and grandchildren who lived with him and visited him every day until he died. In fact, even his daughters-in-law and sons-in-law would drop by the house to check on him and have something to drink with a good conversation.

My first memory of my father dates back to when I was two or three years old. I remember him coming in the door from work; and I would run to him, sit on one of his feet and hold on to his thigh as he walked across the floor in order to give me a ride. Then I would search his pockets for treats like Mary Jane candy, root beer barrels, squirrel nut candy and bazooka bubble gum. He would wash up and the family would always have a home-cooked dinner. As I grew older, my father would teach me through storytelling (High John the Conqueror, Brer Rabbit, and slave master with John the slave became live characters in our home), riddles (complicated puzzles with the answers hidden in the tales dazzled us), ballads (seemingly unending Stagolee rhyming), humor (oftentimes he laughed at his own jokes before he gave us the punch lines), commonsense wisdom ("If a hundred people jumped off a cliff claiming they had wings that could fly, would you follow them?"), maxims ("If he has that much money, why doesn't he take care of his family?"), and laws ("If you take the time to study a thing long enough, you can fix any problem").

In a similar way I was taught by his affirmations. No matter how small my accomplishment, he usually had a positive word to say. I remember once around the age of ten or eleven, I had been out in the woods playing, chasing squirrels, climbing trees, running, picking and eating fruit and nuts, looking for snakes, resting on a ground of clovers while imagining cloud designs, and listening to the silence of the trees and the sounds of birds and leaves. Eventually as the sun moved toward 6 p.m., I started on the way home to be there in time for family dinner. On this occasion I didn't come home empty-handed. In fact, I brought back a small branch with a unique design. My father commented how different this important find was, and I placed the small branch or big twig in the pantry, the room after the kitchen that led to the side of the house. When we got up the next morning and opened the pantry door, about one hundred flying critters flooded the room. The interesting design of my branch/twig had actually been cocoons that birth during the night. My father laughed and laughed as we struggled to run them out of the house through the pantry door to the outdoors. From that boisterous and playful father-son war running the flying invaders out of our house, I grew a sense that it was all right to experiment with the unique, to dabble with the unknown, and even unexpected results became a fun process of correction and rearranging of space and time.

My father bought me my first dictionary when I was in elementary school, and he clearly favored the importance of education. Education functioned as a service to one's family and community. He saw so many resources and opportunities, and usually this became one of his occasional laments about, as he phrased it, "young people today." He held the long view of history and could compare old days when he made do and made a path where there was no path. But in contrast in the current generation, abundant possibilities looked squarely in the faces of youth and young adults. Without an education, how could a man care for his wife and children? Without taking advantage of opportunities, the same question pushed with even more urgency. Actually, my father encouraged all his children and grandchildren to retire early, work for themselves, or start their own business. As his father owned businesses, my father produced sons, sons-in-law, daughters-in-law, grandsons, granddaughters, and great-grandsons who own their own businesses.

When I finished Harvard University, I decided to take a year off to do volunteer work before going to business school; my passion since Kindergarten had been to become a writer, travel the world, make friends, and do business deals. However, that one year of volunteer service turned into five, and my plan to do global investment banking post–business school, changed into enrollment in theological seminary. Because of my father's insight, still I've always related to people involved in business or possessed with a business sense. My closest female friend from the sixth through twelfth grade eventually grew up to own her own cross-country business. My closest female friend at university eventually earned an MBA. My closest female friend during my time in graduate school went on to earn an MBA. And my closest female friend today has an MBA. Hindsight is twenty-twenty and only in the last 9 years have I been able to connect these dots.

Similar to education and businesses, my father also saw church with the same function—to develop the blood family ties of each member in the congregation. Family served as the foundation supported by education, business ownership, and church. These three got their value from their usefulness. As he emphasized in his everyday wisdom, if you stabilize especially the men in those families, then each block of the community gets better, each city and state improve, and the country as a whole becomes a good place to raise children.

My father lived this the best ways he knew how. For instance, one of my father's sons had my father's grandson, and this grandson had my father's great-grandson. (Remember; he died at age ninety-five.) When the great-grandson played little-league football, he could look up into the stands and see watching him his father, his grandfather, and his great-grandfather: four generations of fathers and sons and husbands and husbands-to-be. That great-grandson grew up to do a stint in the National Football League and now owns his own business.

This enduring mountain, my father, did not have an immediate physical, charismatic presence in a room. He was prematurely bald, shorter than I am, with high yellow to white skin color. A quiet man and not one for saying much. But he got things done and worked all the time, fixing his house and car and truck, gardening in the backyard, and keeping the door open for his family and neighbors who wanted to drop by to rest and talk or quench their thirst. My father never smoked or drank, so they would have to settle for coffee, tea, water, or soda. He led four generations by example. Most clearly we experienced this during Christmas time. Until his death at ninety-five, all family members, children (grand- and great-grand-) came back home to my father's house. As long as he was alive, I never missed Christmas with him in Richmond, no matter where in the country or world I might be. It was especially during this holiday that his offspring would participate in a Hopkins ritual of bringing our children to him so that our babies could sit on his lap. Sometimes he held the baby or bounced or made his folk wisdom predictions about what the child would grow up to look like and be. His house buzzed like a beehive as different generations jammed into his home for the holiday ongoing meals, homemade drinks, outlandish gossip, usual picture taking, and full-bodied laughter.

My father, as I mentioned previously, supported my explorations in leadership and adventure. (This is probably one reason why he bought me my first car when I reached sixteen.) He affirmed my participation in the Boy Scouts. I was about to become an eagle scout but I left unfulfilled my final requirements because he wanted me to have a better education and agreed that I should go to an all-boys' boarding school from the second through the sixth form (from eighth through twelfth grade). The summer before I started Groton School (on 415 acres of livable woods) in Massachusetts, I spent eight weeks taking college courses at Dartmouth College in Hanover, New Hampshire. Though I was fourteen years old and on my first trip away from home, I saw these new paths as adventures and expanding opportunities for me and my future family. One of the main role models and safety nets during this path of my young journey was my mountain father. The most challenging parts of five years of boarding school were not the all-day, demanding academics and living with sons whose fathers were some of the wealthiest men in the world. Rather, the greatest challenge was being away from my Richmond home. Consequently, as a dutiful son, I called my father all the time, even when I later travelled around the world. Sometimes, I asked him for help on some issue; in other instances, I explored about family history; usually, we simply had small talk. Despite my high-octane education from an elite boarding school away from home, despite an Ivy League, Harvard University education, despite two PhD degrees and global travels, my leading duty as son was to honor my father until he physically left the earth.

I've often wondered about the factors creating my father's personality, including his deep commitment to his family and his sense of service to others beyond blood ties. I remember an incident when a little boy was in the neighborhood but his mother had left him. My father had his two daughters take in the boy child, give him a bath, clean his dirty clothes, and fill him with food and drink. Similarly, for quite some time, I thought my father had seven sons (including me). But eventually I realized that the seventh son, who spent so much time with us playing, eating, and hanging out during family holidays, was a close family friend. Relatedly, other little children in the neighborhood would come by during the many times my father sat on his front porch and would ask him if he needed anything from the corner store. Although my father didn't really want some groceries, he knew these little ones really wanted to make some extra money. The neighborhood children understood that "Mr. Hopkins" always gave good tips when someone did an errand for him.

Three habits come to mind clarifying my father's everyday living path. First, he regularly sat on the front porch from one to three hours looking out into air, sky, earth, sound, and wind. At a young age, I tried to imitate him, but I couldn't last more than twenty minutes, maybe a half hour. How could he be silent for so long, and what was he watching? I know now he was slowing down the history of life and looking into the not-yet future of tomorrow. During these spiritual practices, my father did not see life in time segments. For him, each moment merely served the purpose of placing him in another reality. And he maintained his deep breathing.

Second, every year since I had left Richmond to go to boarding school at age fourteen, my father would ask, "Dwight, when you gonna go deer hunting with me?" Now with my exposure to northern Yankee, liberal bourgeois culture, how could a modern man indulge in such stuff as killing animals? Each autumn, like clockwork, my father would pose the question, and like clockwork I'd answer, "Maybe next year, Daddy," though I had no intention of participating in such an out-dated and crude ritual of killing innocent deer. Even in his eighties, my father still hunted. Because I guessed he might not live much longer, one year I thought I'd give him this last chance of hunting together. Out in the stillness of the woods, we, father (the oldest) and son (the youngest child), sat with our shotguns (his an automatic and mine a manual pump) in the woods on our deer stand together for two hours. Our bodies did not move. We did not talk. Father and son sat immobile, in absolute silence until I could hear the leaves crackle and could distinguish between the footsteps of squirrels and birds. I saw clouds become one with overhanging branches. I noticed the gentle cool wind moving on all parts of my body. I followed the rhythm of my breathing and how it seemed at peace with the energy of nature. And though I never turned around, I felt the presence of my father sitting about five feet behind me to my left. Through the rhythm of my breathing, my father being there, and the peace of nature's little revelations, I realized how the twenty-five yearly invitations of going hunting were not mainly about killing a deer. Rather, my father wanted me to experience life with him. Indeed, it was a bonding spiritual practice of my self, my father, earth, air, wind, and my imagination of the cosmos.

My third enlightenment about my father came in my interviews of him. When he turned eighty, I tape-recorded him because I didn't know how much longer he had on this side of living. He continued to breathe for some time, and my second recorded interview took place when he had reached ninety. My primary purpose was to record his nearly one hundred years of being on earth in order to capture it for my children, grandchildren and great-grandchildren, as well as for the current and future endless offspring of my father. During that final interview, I asked him what were the keys to his longevity. He answered with a three-part recipe for good being. He responded: "I have that old-time religion, where God will make a way out of no way. BUT God helps those who help themselves." Second, he concluded, "I enjoy each present moment of life." And third, he said, "Every now and then, I like a good sense of humor."

My father represented a man who had harmony and balance of his energy inside of his body. The key was connecting intentional awareness of his breathing with deliberate meditation. In the slow breathing, the rest of his body could rest, and his mind could empty itself so that nature, history, and the future could refill it. In this sense, the harmony and balance of his internal energy reached out or relaxed and accepted the harmony and balance of nature found in each moment of breathing. Christians call this life energy in breath the Holy Spirit; Hindus call it Shakti; African traditional religions call it the presence of the ancestors; and Daoists call it Qi. For my father, Qi stretched back many generations beyond his father William, his grandfather John, through his own 1907 birth, into and beyond the four generations he had produced before he stopped breathing. Harmony and balance of the life energy in his breathing helped the slowing down of life to connect with all surrounding life energy. He had this daily heightened feeling and knowledge for the memory of his forefathers and foremothers and for his current and future children. Thus, the Holy Spirit or Qi mandated duty: do one's family duty daily and the rest is left to heaven.

When he stopped breathing at ninety-five, I was almost fifty. And so, I, the son, had him, the father, for about a half of a century.

Thus my father left a tradition of how to self-cultivate a healthy individual male in relation to producing a healthy community. Indeed, even when he died, he continued his duty to his children: he left us land and money. It is, therefore, that spirituality of self-responsibility and family obligations guiding the collected essays of this volume, *Black Theology—Essays on Gender Perspectives*.

Chapters in the Book

In 1966, a group of forty-eight black American ordained clergy and religious leaders began the process of creating a contemporary black liberation theology. "Theology" refers to a rootedness in the Christian tradition. "Liberation" highlights the main purpose of the historical Jesus (i.e., to liberate workers, the poor, and the emotionally bruised). And "black" acknowledges that theology and liberation reveal themselves in the concrete culture of African American experiences on earth. My first PhD compares black theology in the United States of America with black theology in South Africa. Thus I became a second-generation black liberation theologian. The essays of this volume flow out of that context.

Part One ("The Black Man and Gender Studies") focuses on how black theology sees the creation of the black male gender. It begins with an essay comparing and contrasting the creation of black male leadership represented by Barack H. Obama and Jeremiah A. Wright. The two types of leadership, the chapter argues, complement each other. I presented the core of this essay at the Willamette University Center for Religion and Law and Democracy, on October 23, 2008, a couple of weeks before the first election of Obama as president of the United States. The second essay ("A New Black Heterosexual Male") appeared in *Global Voices for Gender Justice* (2001), a book I coedited with Ramathate Dolamo (South Africa) and Ana Maria Tepedino (Brazil).[1] I see the need to support the black male heterosexual self while accepting varieties of created genders. Multiple truths coexist. "Poor Brother, Rich Brother: Faith, Family, and Education" (1991)[2] stands as my first published article. Indeed, from high school through graduate education until now, the two persisting themes of gender and the global continue in my work.[3] Section 1 concludes with "The Construction of the Black Male Body: Eroticism & Religion" (2004)[4] (with the mixing of religion, eroticism, and the black American male body) and "L.A. and the City: What's God Got To Do with It?" (1994),[5] which explains the 1991, Los Angeles, Rodney King affair as a symbol for America's opinion of the black male experience.

Part Two ("The Black Man and Black Women") presents a black theology influenced by black women's practice, thinking, dreaming, and believing. To that end, chapter 6—"Black Theology of Liberation and the Impact of Womanist Theology" (2002)[6]—acknowledges how much black liberation

1. Pilgrim Press, 2001; reprint, Eugene, OR: Wipf & Stock, 2007.
2. In *Amazing Grace!* October 1991.
3. On the global, see Hopkins, *Black Theology: Essays on Global Perspectives* (Eugene, OR: Cascade Books, 2017).
4. In *Loving the Body: Black Religious Studies and the Erotic* (New York: Palgrave Macmillan, 2004), 179–97. I am a coeditor.
5. Keynote opening address of the First Annual Pan African Religious Studies Center, the School of Theology at Claremont, Claremont, California.
6. Found in my book *Heart and Head: Black Theology Past, Present, and Future* (New York: Palgrave, 2002).

theology has learned from the pioneering work of womanist thought leaders and their practice. "Womanist Gardens & Lives above Suspicion" (2006), chapter 7,[7] shows my acceptance of a womanist invitation to reflect on how their school of thinking impacted my worldview. Chapter 8, "Enslaved Black Women: A Theology of Justice and Reparations" (2010)[8] is my response to an invitation from a feminist scholar who hosted an international conference on overcoming the religious and sexual legacy of slavery. "Black Women's Spirituality of Funk" (1993), chapter 9, explores what theological, political, and cultural lessons can we learn from the fictional characters in Toni Morrison's first five novels.[9] The last chapter ("Black and Womanist Theologies," 2010) is my introduction to the papers from the first and, so far, only national, cosponsored black theology and womanist theology conference consisting of theological educators, pastors, and religious leaders.[10]

With more and more younger and second-career students entering graduate schools of religious education and training, and with growing popular interests in religion and its relation to real human conditions of people who walk on the physical earth, I decided to pull together this collection of essays. I have edited previously published essays and added a new speech. In addition, my domestic and global travels have impressed upon me a continual curiosity and ongoing openness to learn about black liberation theology. As one contribution to that theological trend, this book stands as a one-stop shop, so to speak, for my views on black theology exploring the vibrant topic of gender studies.

Hopefully *Black Theology—Essays on Gender Perspectives* will spark your memory and imagination on how to form a healthy individual within a healthy community. We are all in this thing together, trying to lift up legacies, affirm traditions, and apply fluidity and innovation of the now as we look at least three generations into the future. Black theology and gender studies remain one strand within a larger story of the United States and, in fact, among all the peoples of the world talking story.

---

7. In Stacey M. Floyd-Thomas, ed., *Deeper Shades of Purple: Womanism in Religion and Society*, Religion, Race, and Ethnicity (New York: New York University Press, 2006), 282–89.

8. In Bernadette Brooten, ed., *Beyond Slavery: Overcoming Its Religious and Sexual Legacies* (New York: Palgrave Macmillan, 2010).

9. It represents a modified condensing of chapter 2 in my *Shoes That Fit Our Feet: Sources for a Constructive Black Theology* (Maryknoll, NY: Orbis, 1993).

10. In *Walk Together Children: Black and Womanist Theologies, Church and Theological Education* (Eugene, OR: Cascade Books, 2010): I am the lead editor of this volume.

Part 1:
The Black Man and Gender Studies

1

Two Black Male Leaders: Barack Obama and Jeremiah Wright

One of the fascinating developments in the 2008 presidential election has been the discussions of black religion and black theology in the debate. For instance, on February 10, 2007, Illinois State Senator Barack Obama announced his candidacy for the White House. Shortly after, the *New York Times* published a March 2007 article that suggested that Obama was beginning to distance himself from his pastor, Rev. Jeremiah A. Wright Jr., and that Obama might be linked to a radical form of black Christianity. Occasionally throughout 2007, some corporate media attempted to link Rev. Wright with Minister Louis Farrakhan. Because Rev. Wright was Obama's pastor, then, in the logic of some corporate media, Obama was connected to Farrakhan. Wright and Obama seemed to represent two models of black male leadership.

Yet the controversy did not gain traction until the beginning of 2008. On Thursday, March 13, 2008, America and the world woke up to an amazing media production. On that day, ABC television released a thirty-second sound bite from three of Rev. Wright's sermons. The public saw ten seconds each of three sermon excerpts. By the next day, Friday the fourteenth, the number-one American presidential news in the U.S., and increasingly globally, were the following questions: How could Senator Obama have such an angry, racist-in-reverse, nonpatriotic black pastor; and was this the form of black religion that Obama believed in?

Not only did some corporate media, Republican candidates, and Senator Hillary Clinton begin to raise questions about Obama. But the very base of his campaign supporters became shocked. On that Friday on the blog of BarackObama.com, one could find some of Obama's staunchest supporters trembling in confusion, fear, and suspicion. It seemed as if Obama's ground troops were disintegrating. In fact, the arguing and the anger on that website was so deep that some Obama supporters were accusing other bloggers of being Hillary Clinton trolls. A troll is a supporter of one presidential candidate who posts on an opposing candidate's blog or website in order to cause disruption and sow false information among that candidate's core supporters.

On that Friday afternoon, I was in the Fox News studio about to go on live television when one of the reporters called me over and said that he was printing a major news development. We waited for the printer to stop. Then he handed me a statement by Senator Obama. Obama announced in this brief press release that he denounced the thirty-second sound bites and that he was not present when they were preached. I went on television; and of course the first question I was asked was, Did I agree with "God damn America" and that "9/11 meant chickens coming home to roost"?

Over that weekend, a political storm unfolded, and the domestic and global media looped the thirty-second sound bites over and over. The following Tuesday, I was in the NPR (National Public Radio) studio doing a live interview when our program was cut short because Obama was about to begin a live broadcast. Everyone hurried to the back of the studio where six TV monitors hung on the walls. I grabbed a seat on the floor and watched Obama's "A More Perfect Union" speech. Standing in Philadelphia, draped in American flags, Obama gave his first major speech on race, religion, and the black church.

Still the uproar persisted. Every day for about three weeks I did television, radio, magazine, newspaper, and web interviews on the topic of black religion, the black church, and black theology of liberation. During one of those weeks, I had to cancel and reschedule classes for a later date due to media interview requests. My e-mail box and the voicemail boxes for my home phone and cell phone were filling up. I did media from 9 a.m. to 10 p.m. for those seven days. The questions of reporters began to repeat themselves: What is black religion, what is the black church, and what is black liberation theology?

These requests continued for several weeks. However, as the country and the world moved away from the initial thirty-second sound bites, the media questions started to ask for a more sophisticated explanation.

Then Rev. Wright announced a major press conference at the National Press Club in Washington, DC. On Monday, April 28, I sat at a VIP table in front of the podium as Rev. Wright gave his statement and then participated in the now famous question-and-answer session. Immediately, Senator Obama held his own press conference where he condemned Wright's remarks and stated that for him, Obama, Wright did not represent the black church known by Obama. Here the leading Democratic presidential candidate and probably the first black American president in United States history placed black religion, the black church, and black theology of liberation at the center of American and global political discussions. Clearly the black church as an invisible institution had become visible for all to see.

From Friday March 14, 2008, until March 2009, I had been on different media outlets—the major U.S. corporate media, independent media, local media, and on media interviews from Africa, Asia, the Caribbean, Canada, South America, and Europe. What is clear to me is a need for a nationwide conversation on black religion, the black church, and black liberation theology.

What Is Black Liberation Theology?

To understand the phrase "black theology of liberation" or "black liberation theology," it is helpful to define each of the three words in the phrase. The term *theology* means that black theology of liberation is rooted in the Christian tradition. That is to say, Christianity begins with the historical Jesus, through the disciples of the early church, and its eventual spread throughout church tradition of the last two thousand years. The word *liberation* in "black theology of liberation" represents a belief that the framework, ministry, and orientation of Jesus is liberation. And the word *black* answers the question of how do theology and liberation look in African American culture. Thus black liberation theology is focused on three themes. It is rooted in the Christian tradition, wedded to the gospel of liberation, and revealed in black culture.

Though these three themes can be found in the origin and historical development of black religion and the black church since slavery in the United States, the specific phrase "black theology of liberation," is a recent creation. It arose in the 1960s.

Specifically, on July 31, 1966, a group of African American pastors and church administrators published a full-page advertisement in the *New York Times*. This ad was called the "Black Power" statement. And, it actually supported the new agenda of black power. The ad was a direct response to the cry of Black Power that Stokely Carmichael made on June 16, 1966. Black Power was a bold move on the part of the youth wing of the civil rights movement. It spread throughout society and forced various groups to respond.

The black clergy who published the ad were caught in a dilemma. As Christian pastors who were staunch participants in Martin Luther King Jr.'s nonviolent civil rights movement, they were now confronted with a fundamental question in America: What does blackness have to do with the gospel of Jesus Christ? In a word, was it possible to be both black and Christian? This was the defining question which black theology answered.

As these young African American pastors and church administrators thought about this question, others were already giving their answers.

At that time, many in America gave a negative response to the question. They believed that a person could not be both black and Christian. Many in the white community associated the Black Power movement with terrorism, racism in reverse, Malcolm X, and law-breaking radicals—unpatriotic militants waiving guns against the status quo. How could this type of "blackness" be linked to the religion of Jesus? In addition, the black community had its doubters as well.

For instance, Malcolm X and the Nation of Islam said people could not be both Christian and black because Christianity was the white man's religion. It was the religion used by white citizens to enslave Africans. It justified and supported slavery for almost three centuries in North America. It was a religion that gave blacks a pacifist Jesus and a hope in heaven by and by while white Christians had their heaven on earth. Christianity, for Malcolm X, was white supremacy tricknology.

Black militants and revolutionaries such as the Black Panther Party said that Christianity was a deadly addiction for black people, suited for Negro uncle toms. Negro preachers were sellouts, who fed on the financial insecurity of poor people. Power might have to grow out of the barrel of a gun and not from a hocus-pocus Christian Bible.

Black artists used poetry and fiction to show how Christianity blocked the flourishing of the new African and African American culture with its emphasis on Egypt and African traditional spirituality.

Coming from the perspective of supporting Christianity, Martin Luther King Jr. and his preacher colleagues also stated that one could not be black and Christian. They believed that Christianity was a nonviolent, love-your-enemy, and turn-the-other-cheek religion. In radical contrast, they felt that black power was violence and hatred. So one could not be black and Christian. King believed that one could be Negro and Christian, but not black and Christian.

We know that the civil rights movement begins December 1, 1955, in Montgomery, Alabama, with the boycott and Dr. King leading that boycott. And the black church, particularly in the South, is the leadership of the civil rights movement, is the leadership of the voting rights and human rights movement there. In the North, there was a different reality, and a lot of the issues that blacks in the South and their allies were fighting for did not match experiences of blacks in ghettos and the nitty-gritty intensity of being black in the North.

But even when the African American church was leading struggles in the South, it came to a point where a younger generation of Negro youth, which eventually changed to black youth, became very dissatisfied with the pace of the black church and with some of the theology and interpretation of Christianity of Dr. King and his lieutenants in his organization, the Southern Christian Leadership Conference. So the pace of the struggle, the message of the struggle, and even how Dr. King and some of the black clergy in the South were relating to the federal government—all these factors forced the youth wing of the civil rights movement, particularly led by Stokely Carmichael, to become very frustrated with what they were experiencing. They wanted their justice. They wanted their civil rights. They wanted their power now. And so they created the phrase "black power" in 1966.

That is why the following question came to the surface: Okay, if the black church is being discredited in the North, and if the black church is being discredited in the South, then what is the role of Christianity or religion in social justice for the Negro revolution, as it was first called, and eventually for the black-power consciousness revolution?

In the midst of this national firestorm over race, religion, and the future of America, black pastors and church administrators, led by James H. Cone, resolved the question, could one be both black and Christian?

In March of 1969, James H. Cone published his first book called *Black Theology and Black Power*. In this text, Cone stated that the message of the gospel is liberation. Jesus, in Cone's view, had one purpose. He came to liberate the poor, the oppressed, and those emotionally abused. Similarly, black people were poor, oppressed, and emotionally abused. They, like Jesus, were organizing for liberation. So if the purpose of Jesus was for the liberation of the oppressed, and oppressed black citizens were struggling for liberation, then it followed that Jesus worked in oppressed black communities for liberation. If these were not true, it would contradict the message of the Bible.

Dr. Cone comes into the picture and begins to explain how one can still be Christian on the one hand and also be relevant to the new movement of black power and black consciousness on the other. And so he wrote that first book, *Black Theology and Black Power*, which basically said, "Aha! There is no contradiction between the social justice movement of black power and civil rights and the message of Jesus Christ. In fact, black power is for liberation. Jesus Christ is for liberation. And not only is Christianity not an enemy of black power, but black power is the contemporary expression of Jesus Christ in America."

With his theological interpretation and his read of the sociology of America, Cone stated that the message of Jesus was not the opposite of black power. Quite the contrary: black power was the message of Jesus for all of America.

And one could imagine with that conclusion that all hell broke loose. For instance, Cone was attacked by professors and universities and seminaries. Mainstream media came out and attacked his book because they felt that black power plus black theology meant violence. They argued intensely that it attacked the gospel of Jesus. They raised questions: how could someone challenge the authority of not turning the other cheek and not telling black people to suffer quietly as their oppressor beat them to a bloody pulp? Others screamed out criticisms that black theology of liberation was mixing politics with religion. Some stated that it was simply an ideological movement on the part of this young radical James Cone with a huge Afro hairstyle. For them, Cone and his theology were not the quiet, well-groomed, and law-abiding Martin Luther King Jr. On the contrary, the founders of black theology argued that poor black people had the right to interpret the Bible for themselves.

The problem that the mainstream professors in schools, the mainstream churches, and the broader U.S. society had with black theology is that it combined the word *black* with the word *theology*.

In fact, Dr. King mentioned that perhaps it should have been Negro power, or Negro theology, and he spoke specifically to Stokely Carmichael about this. He said, "You know, Stokely, why do you have to put the word black in front of power? And why not Negro or something like that? You know, it's important for Negroes and blacks to have power, but why do you have to connect those two words so closely together?"

We have to remember: in the 1960s a lot of people in the United States, including black people in the black community, were just getting the *N* capitalized in the word *Negro*. They were just getting used to even using the word "Negro," instead of the previous term, "colored people." And now Stokely Carmichael and the youth wing of the civil rights movement just stated, "We're going to skip all of that 'colored to negro' stuff. We're going to go right to black. And not only are we going to go right to black, we're going to add power to black." Of course, the word *power* raised a variety of questions. Does that power mean Malcolm X? Does it mean militant underground movements? Does it mean some alliance with Africa? What is this power and why does it have to be black?

Because black theology came out of the civil rights movement and even more so from the youth wing (led by Stokley Carmichael and the black consciousness and black power part of the civil rights movement), most of the mainstream authorities in the church and broader society described the militant madness of Carmichael and how this militant madness was now entering the black church and its theology. Mainstream authorities believed that if black power was against white people, then black theology must be against the white church.

But for Cone and the founders of black liberation theology, Jesus came to save the whole person—that is to say, both the soul and the body; salvation comes in the personal, spiritual realm and in the public, structural realm. In fact, the word *salvation* meant liberation from oppression of internal spiritual pain and from the oppression of external systematic pain.

Thus the key to black theology of liberation is not primarily the idea of being black. Rather, it is the interpretation of Jesus and the Bible.

First, the Bible. Since the March 2007 *New York Times* article on Barack Obama and Jeremiah Wright, many in the media have questioned whether or not black theology of liberation is a recent historical fad, an outmoded outcry, or an anti-Christian ideology.

What these questions have in common is a confusion over how black theology of liberation comes out of the Christian Bible. They have not understood how the Bible itself touches on political issues. Because the Bible is the foundation and the substance of black theology of liberation and because the Bible touches on politics, black theology also touches on politics. For example, in the Old Testament, there is one thread that holds this entire text together. It is a story of how Yahweh God made a covenant of liberation and freedom with the ancient Israelites, who were physically in slavery, physically in chains. God saw their broken bodies. And God decided to take a political stance by fighting against the political state of Pharaoh.

Yahweh defeats Pharaoh's public policy of slavery and helps the ancient Israelites to achieve liberation. It is a political liberation where former slaves, with God's leadership, are freed from the power structure of Pharaoh. Then, based on Yahweh's promise, they pursue a political goal—the establishment of their own liberated, free political state. In fact, every year Jewish brothers and sisters celebrate Passover. This ritual reminds them that their ancestors used to be in physical slavery. And that Yahweh worked with them to liberate them from Pharaoh's oppression. In addition, the establishment of the state of Israel in May 1948 shows that the Hebrew Scriptures (or Old Testament) touch on political liberation.

When we turn to the Christian Scriptures or New Testament, we see that black theology of liberation is also a representation of Jesus. In fact, Jesus carries out the liberation tradition of the Old Testament. We must remember that Jesus was not a Christian; he was Jewish. When we focus on

Jesus's words as recorded in the Bible, the political aspects of Jesus's message become clear.

A question comes up: Are Jesus's words and life political? All agree that Jesus offered profound spiritual salvation and liberation from negative emotions and mean-spiritedness. What about his relations to political state power? At least two passages point to political liberation on the part of Jesus.

The book of Luke chapters 3 and 4 show how Jesus was baptized, a ritual symbolizing his preparation to deal with spiritual and systemic evil on earth. After the baptism, the very next passage in the Bible tells a story of how Jesus was immediately tempted by evil power. The plot shows how Jesus overcame all negative temptations. Fortified by baptism and having defeated earthly and spiritual forces, Jesus's next move is to clarify what is his mission on earth. Here we find his beginning speech or sermon, his first public address to the world. This is the first and clearest story of Jesus's earthly mission, why he has come to human beings. It answers the question about the one, primary reason why Jesus was born and what is the essential purpose of Christianity. What is his mission on earth? What should all of his followers do?

The response appears in the book of Luke chapter 4 where we find one of the most famous and one of the most decisive passages in the New Testament. It tells us what Jesus's primary mission is to humankind and all creation. Jesus says his principal mission calls him to bring good news to the poor, to proclaim release to the captives, to give sight to the blind, and to give liberty to those who are oppressed. The very earthly dimension of his one purpose confronts readers in quite a striking way. We discover no reference to a hocus-pocus religion. Rather, the story has Jesus placing spiritual matters within material earthly concerns. In other words, the purpose of Jesus touches on the whole human purpose—a spirituality completely tied to the oppression and liberation of human beings on earth now.

In addition, when Jesus followed his essential mission, he ran into the state machinery of Rome. The political authority of Rome executed Jesus because he would not bow down to false earthly gods and he would not worship the Roman emperor as God. Rather he preached that a new and higher authority had power over Rome. But some will say that Jesus was not political because he did not practice politics. Actually, politics is not so much defined by people who call themselves political. What makes a person political is whether or not the state machinery moves against and attacks him.

Jesus revealed politics at two levels, at least. (1) He tried to liberate poor and working-class people who had been made that way by the Roman colonizers. And (2) the Roman colonizers used their political power to eliminate a potential power that claimed to be greater than the Roman occupying government. If Jesus had not been a political threat, the political state would not have lynched him on an old tree.

In the book of Matthew chapter 25, verses 31 to 46, we discover another one of the most important commands of Jesus. Through the millennia, it remains a key decisive instruction from Jesus because, in the sixty-six books of the Protestant Bible, this story appears to be the only place where Jesus gives absolute orders on how to get to heaven. In Christian doctrine, the purpose of Christians is to have hope in a new life, a new reality for themselves and their children and grandchildren. This never ending hope for change is the beauty of Christianity. Here in Matthew's story, Jesus lays out the primary criteria for this hope in a new life. It is the duty of Christians to follow these criteria and this mission given by the founder of Christianity. In Matthew, Jesus provides the criteria and mission for the only way Christians can get into heaven. They carry out that mission when they do the following: feed the hungry, give drink to the thirsty, welcome the stranger, clothe the naked, take care for the sick, and visit those in prison.

It is no accident that the primary mission announced in Jesus's public address in Luke is the same mission for Christians announced in Matthew. The purpose of Jesus and the purpose of Christians is to liberate the oppressed.

Again, black theology of liberation arose out of a social context that corresponded with the purpose and mission of Jesus. Black theology touches on politics because Jesus touched on politics.

In addition to black theology using themes from the Bible, the origin of the African American church in the United States is another source for the development of a contemporary black liberation theology. The birth of the black church in North America was a spiritual and political movement against the legal economic and political rule of a Christian white power. The official U.S. federal and state public policies supported human slavery. Therefore, enslaved black people in the eighteenth and nineteenth centuries believed that slavery contradicted the purpose and mission of Jesus.

In the South during slavery, the black church functioned underground; consequently, scholars have called it the Invisible Institution. An active political organization and movement, it aggressively opposed the state's slave politics. It pursued the goals of redistributing power, obtaining equal rights, and activating full citizenship. The southern black church organized against state politics. And they prayed to their God to set them free from both spiritual and structural evil. Late at night, blacks would sneak away to an appointed cabin, or go down in the swamps and ravines, or build brush harbors deep in the woods, or stretch out in the corn rows—all to hope for a better day for their children on earth in the United States. Black churches were separated not only because their religion of liberation differed from the slave masters'. They secretly built their own institutions because they were tired of sitting outside of a white church service or being forced to gather in segregated sections of white churches. Thus the black church in the South opposed the government's supporting policy of racial segregation. They did this by breaking the law, meeting secretly, and mixing preaching with the politics of liberation.

Furthermore, the northern black church arose under similar conditions with similar institutional purpose. In 1787 in Philadelphia, the founders of the republic wrote the U.S. Constitution. Coincidently and ironically, in that very same year in the very same city, the northern independent black church was born.

At that time, a black man named Richard Allen and others were members of the segregated section of St. George's Methodist Episcopal Church in Philadelphia. One Sunday in church, Richard Allen was trying to make his way to the segregated section. But someone up front began to pray. In most churches, when someone starts a prayer, everyone, out of respect for the prayer, stops where he or she is. Allen stopped when he heard the prayer start. But he was physically interrupted in his prayer when some men forcefully removed him. Unfortunately, Allen had stopped to pray in the segregated white section. Out of this incident, Richard Allen went on to found the African Methodist Episcopal Church—the AME. Like their southern brothers and sisters, these northerners built their own independent black church in response to political, state-sponsored segregation.

At least these two sources—Jesus in the Bible and the history of the African American church—were foundations of the black theology of liberation in the late 1960s.

We remember that the creators of today's black theology were pastors of churches and church administrators. They were leaders rooted in African American communities and neighborhoods. As mentioned earlier, they wanted to know if it was possible to be both black and Christian. And they wanted to know if God was present in the 1960s crisis of race in America. Was God involved in personal salvation and social justice, liberation of the soul and the body? Was their God concerned about the whole person?

The importance of James H. Cone's March 1969 book, *Black Theology and Black Power*, is that it gave a theological response to these questions. Cone and the founders of black theology did not operate in a vacuum. In April of 1968, Martin Luther King, Jr. had been assassinated. In response, riots were raging all across America. Many in the black community were finished with following Christianity and the black church. With King's death, they believed that Christianity and the church were not only irrelevant to the freedom of oppressed people, but they could be possibly supporting the oppression of African American communities.

Many criticized the church as a Negro institution rather than a black gathering for freedom. They believed that if the nonviolent, Christian way of King had been killed, then it was time to look for something new. To fill the void, many in the black community, including some churches, began to turn to African political movements and African culture and spirituality. Others took a closer look at the different organizations within the black power movement. Still others explored the possibility of more militant avenues.

Again, what Cone's book and the new black theology of liberation did was to tell a whole generation of young people that they did not have to leave church and seek other avenues. They answered the question that one did not have to be a Negro. Rather, one could be both black and Christian. Their efforts helped many to stay with Christianity and stay within the church.

Trinity United Church of Christ in Chicago

During 1971, one of the churches struggling with how to live out the theological conclusion that a person could be both black and Christian was Trinity United Church of Christ on the South Side of Chicago. During that year, they only had eighty-seven members. At that time, they decided not to leave the urban area and move to the suburbs. Rather, they chose to try and build on their understanding of the Bible's salvation and liberation right in the oppressed inner city of Chicago.

When the church concluded that it would give its life to the poor and workers of the South Side, it hired Jeremiah A. Wright Jr. in March 1972. The eighty-seven-member congregation told him to apply a relevant gospel to black culture and the economic and political plight of black Americans. Through focusing on these forgotten citizens of America, the church hoped to redeem the soul of all of America.

Under Wright's leadership, members of the surrounding community and others from faraway neighborhoods began to join Trinity. He was successful in bringing in families and also black men back into the church.

By 1981, Trinity had refined its theological focus. Because it made a conscious decision to relate to the specific conditions of the communities that surrounded it in the Chicago ghettoes, it wrote two statements to fulfill its mission. In other words, the conditions in which the church found itself impacted the specific way the church applied the biblical call for love and liberation in those conditions. The first document is Trinity's statement of self-reflection, which reads:

> We are a congregation which is Unashamedly Black and Unapologetically Christian . . . Our roots in the Black religious experience and tradition are deep, lasting and permanent. We are an African people, and remain 'true to our native land,' the mother continent, the cradle of civilization. God has superintended our pilgrimage through the days of slavery, the days of segregation, and the long night of racism. It is God who gives us the strength and courage to continuously address injustice as a people, and as a congregation. We constantly affirm our trust in God through cultural expression of a Black worship service and ministries which address the Black Community.

The second statement is called The Black Value System and covers eight values: commitment to God, commitment to the black community, commitment to the black family, dedication to the pursuit of education, dedication to the pursuit of excellence, adherence to the black work ethic, commitment to self-discipline and self-respect, and disavowal of the pursuit of "middleclassness."

The first value indicates that like other Christians, members of Trinity had submitted to the leadership of God in the movement for freedom. The second value emphasizes the need to strengthen the black community, which had fallen on hard times. The third value committed the church to strengthen and love the black family. And it also urged all black families to reach out to all those less fortunate. Here is suggested the need for black men to take more responsibility for their families and black parents to take more responsibility for their children.

The fourth value dedicated the church to increase the intellectual and mental potential of all African American people. For Trinity, education had to include elements that produce high school graduates with marketable skills, a trade or qualifications for apprenticeships, or proper preparation for college. Basic education for all blacks would include mathematics, science, logic, general semantics, participative politics, economics and finance, and the care and nurture of black minds.

The fifth value stated that the level of excellence of one year must be exceeded by greater efforts in the following year. The sixth value claimed that high productivity must be the goal of an African American workforce. The seventh value explained how, even if the African American community was exploited by other forces, that community still should have its own self-discipline and self-respect to bring about progress and be positive examples to young people.

And the eighth value places quotation marks around the phrase "middleclassness." Thus the word "middleclassness" refers to a very narrow definition of the middle class. Specifically, the eighth value targets the false goal of focusing only on the talented tenth of the black community. In contrast to only supporting the top 10 percent, progress should also include the poor and working people; that is to say, all of the African American community had to be the focus of Christian activities.

With the young pastor Jeremiah Wright hired, he and the church leaders were able to grow Trinity from eighty-seven to 8,500 members. This was mainly due to their ability to recognize that the Bible had to speak to the oppressed conditions on the South Side of Chicago. The church did not exist in the suburbs or the wealthy downtown areas. A visit to Trinity United Church confirms this observation.

When one drives toward the parking lot of Trinity, it is clear that these Christian believers have made a conscious decision to stay in the inner city or ghetto. Going West on Ninety-Fifth Street, one has to cross the railroad tracks that run next to the church's parking lot and can carry a long train of commercial cars lasting sometime from five to fifteen minutes. In this way, a person can be made late for church because of slow-moving, squealing steel cars.

Already a visitor will experience the connection between time, faith, and commercial interests on the South Side of Chicago. The South Side is the deeply segregated part of Chicago. It is where the city's cross-country businesses route bleak looking trains that interrupt parishioners' attempts to carry out their daily faith by simply crossing tracks to worship. In other words, the time to start church services is ignored by economic interests that send the polluted noise and exhaust of a long train to the black South Side. Being delayed for church means that Ninety-Fifth Street is seen as a wasteland for powerful downtown financial brokers.

Similarly, we see little shops sprinkled here and there on Ninety-Fifth Street—such as a small grocery store, a McDonald's, and a hair care shop. But the low-rent apartments or public housing and the abandoned lots also strike the eye. One gets the sense that hard times have fallen on this part of the world and maybe it is not a place that a parent would necessarily want to raise a child.

In contrast, the North Side, equally segregated, is where a disproportionate number of wealthy whites own two-million-dollar homes nestled on the lovely Lake Michigan. Some of these houses have private in-door swimming pools. Here, kids attend elite private schools or excellent public schools. Politicians hold their million-dollar fundraisers on the North Side.

The South Side is where they come to mobilize black churches to get out the vote. On the North Side, police officers ride bicycles and stop and have ice cream with the public. On the South Side, cops ride two to a car. They show their shotguns and wear the weight of thick bulletproof vests.

Yet it is because of its physical location situated in the semiblighted, forced-segregated reality of poor and working-class black families that thousands of Christians and voyeurs are attracted to Trinity. They come every Sunday and every day of the week for social services and spiritual healing. In fact, its 8,500 members and countless occasional seekers jam into the physical building during three regular services each Sunday: at 7 a.m., 11 a.m., and 6 p.m. At one time there was an additional Saturday evening church service for those who planned to go partying later that night.

Rev. Wright is a formally trained musician and singer. So he also built up Trinity's membership by celebrating music and sacred dance.

Many people joined Trinity because of the spiritual safety of an extended family, and because it preached and practiced a black theology of liberation—a theology interpreting the Bible's concern for the spirit and the material body. As he responded to the instructions of the church committee that hired him, Wright included a deep reading of the Bible, highly educated leadership, evangelical worship services, dozens of ministries for poor communities, strong labor advocacy, ordination of women, welcoming of different sexualities, outreach to Africa and the Third World, and a quick wit and humor in one mixed community.

Trinity was made up of an intimate lively group of inner-city South Siders who were ready for an in-depth educated explanation of the Bible. They really wanted institutions of service to the marginalized communities. They valued the opportunity to create new ways of building a devastated physical area. And they enjoyed an occasional cutting sermon that spoke truth to power and called out names of those who had done wrong in contradiction to their interpretation of the Bible.

Most of Wright's sermons over thirty-six years focused on standard themes from the black inner-city community and family—self-love, self-respect, black men assuming responsibility, the positive African heritage, service to the poor as a Christian way of life, providing the highest education for children, domestic violence, building black girl's self-esteem, HIV and AIDS awareness, acceptance of a sexually diverse creation, a call for those with more resources to share with the lest fortunate, and emphasis on being grounded in the Bible. But occasionally, Wright chose to explain the wrongdoings of the powerful. Of course, he gave his Christian interpretation.

At this point in our discussion, let's go back to the March 13, 2008, bombshell that rocked the presidential election with themes of race, religion, and presidential politics. We remember that ABC Television released a thirty-second sound bite that included ten seconds each of three of Wright's previous sermons. Now Wright had been preaching at Trinity for thirty-six years. Each Sunday, Trinity had held three services. And each Sunday, Wright had preached three new and different sermons. So that meant that of the 1,872 sermons Wright had preached in thirty-six years, the ABC reporter made a conscious decision to take ten seconds from three specific sermons. In other words, out of 7,500 minutes of Wright's sermons, the reporter lifted up thirty seconds of incomplete preaching.

But still, if one reviews each of the ten seconds in the thirty-second sound bite, one might come to a different perspective.

For instance, in the thirty-second sound bite, when Wright mentioned "chickens coming home to roost," he was quoting and paraphrasing Edward Peck. Peck had already given these same conclusions about September 11. This statement about chickens coming home to roost is talking about the idea of blowback violence. In international politics, there's a phrase called "blowback violence." That is to say, a superpower country "perpetrates" violence against a smaller nation. Eventually the smaller nations will come back with their violence. In this sense, that violence "blows back" to the superpower nation.

Also, we must remember that Peck was a former ambassador to Iraq. Peck had been associate director of a presidential antiterrorist department. Peck had been part of the Reagan administration. Peck had given his analysis four days after the 9/11 attacks and one day before Wright delivered his sermon. And Peck was a white man. Ambassador Peck said these words the Saturday after 9/11, and Wright preached similar words the next day, on Sunday.

At the same time, we do have to point out that of course Ambassador Peck did not say it with a certain intensity that we heard in the thirty-second sound bite. Because that's the nature of the black church; it's the good and the bad, the up and the down, the joy and the anger, the pain and the resurrection. All of these emotions are mixed in there together.

Let's look at the other infamous sermonic sound bite of "God damn America." When Wright says "God damn America," he uses a specific pronunciation and accent. He says "*God* damn America." That's different from our popular use of the phrase—excuse my English—"Goddammit." Goddammit is a sort of vulgar popular usage of language in America as a curse. But if you listen, Wright is saying "*God* damn America."

That's a different pronunciation. When Wright briefly mentioned "God damn America," he believed he was following the Hebrew Scripture's prophets. In those texts, Yahweh/God made a covenant with ancient Israel. Israel was given resources and abundance. When Israel strayed from the covenant, Yahweh/God raised up prophets as instruments of God's damnation. The deity used human beings to pronounce divine judgment and religious condemnation on a wayward nation.

The second thing we need to observe is, when Wright says "God damn America," if we listen closely or look closely, he says, "I'm in the Bible. It's in the Bible." Well, actually, he can make a case that he was preaching from the Bible. "Damn" can mean righteous indignation on the part of Yahweh/God; it can mean divine judgment against the people and the people of God. So, actually, as Wright says, in a sense he was still following the Bible. It's just that the national and international audiences that watched the thirty-second sound bite did not see what Wright preached about before the sound bite and after the sound bite. Wright did an analysis of the characters and words in the biblical passage to which he referred, and then he applied his analysis to the wrong policies of the United States government and concluded: God damn America.

In the biblical passage tradition to which he referred, there's a covenant or relationship between Yahweh/God and the ancient people of Israel. And God calls on them to be a special nation, a blessed nation. But if they break the covenant, then the Old Testament prophets (such as Jeremiah and Amos) will come forth and proclaim "thus saith the Lord," and they speak truth to power. God will condemn this nation until it wakes up and then turns toward the original path of justice and peace and positive relationship with all nations in the regions of the Mediterranean Sea. It really is the prophetic task of moving the nation from where it is to the glory that it can be. And a prophet in the Bible gets impatient and can at times express some anger.

Basically, Wright seems to be saying the following: "I'm speaking as a prophet for the word of God and its judgment on America because (a) America hasn't used its resources to help its own oppressed citizens, like African Americans. (b) America hasn't helped working-class people. And (c) America has not used its foreign affairs policies, strength, and leadership to bring about peace. Instead, it has bombed people." Thus on various levels, Wright seems to be urging the nation to move away from that wayward path toward a more just and peace loving path.

The black-church sermon can contain a range of emotions and practices: from damnation to seduction to cunning wit to theatrical performance. And to that degree, Wright was following the African American sermonic outline of five steps to successful preaching.

The first step is where the preacher takes a biblical passage and unpacks that. He or she looks at word studies, the personality and figures in the story, and the context of the narrative. Step 2 is when the preacher meditates and deliberates over this in-depth study and applies it to personal issues of healing: to such issues like HIV and AIDS, domestic violence, the loneliness of single adults, low self-esteem, and other things that keep people from feeling good about themselves. After applying the in-depth study of the Bible to personal emotional concerns, the preacher takes this intensive study of the Bible and applies it to a prophetic message against unjust powers, against structures and systems. This is step 3—divine judgment and condemnation. And then the fourth step brings everything together, and offers the hope of a new life both for the individual and the nation. Here the preacher tells the congregation the following: "Now that you've gone through the horrendous nights of your personal issues, and the intensity of systems oppressing you, our next question is, how do we become complete persons—individually, psychically, emotionally, and systemically as a person, as a people, as a nation, and as a world? And that's because God loves us."

And at the fifth and final step, the preacher tells the congregation that it can enter a new community of God's love. That is why in the majority of black churches, the preacher ends with these words: the doors of the church are open; please enter.

So what we have in the thirty-second sound bite of Jeremiah Wright is a jump over steps 1 and 2 and the absence of steps 4 and 5. Rather, the sound bite shows step 3—the preacher prophet pointing out to the nation its wayward ways. We only see judgment. But the best flow of black preaching always invites the listener to the hope of change of the self and change of systems.

Race and Life Experiences

Because Barack Obama was not present at Trinity United Church of Christ during the thirty-second sound bite aired by ABC, he condemned what he saw on television. However, I think it is not only that Obama was not in the congregation when Wright preached these sermons. I also think each man had different encounters with race and different life experiences. As a result, they together present two models for black male leadership.

Barack Obama is white and black and immigrant and multicultural.

Genetically white and intimately nurtured in American white culture, in this sense Obama is white. His mother and his grandparents came from a white, heartland America and semirural America. Growing up with a white mother and white grandparents, Obama caught a glimpse of how many white citizens expect society and government to respond to their needs. Socialization processes in the United States (i.e., the family, media, education, movies, and power positions) can help white citizens imagine whatever options they wish to choose in life. Not only can one see different options, but one can also decide to implement and, thus, realize those dreams. Despite his grandmother mentioning her fears of inner-city black people, Obama grew up in a predominantly white environment that nurtured a view of government and American citizens as working together so each citizen could realize his/her desires. This perspective leads to a career as a politician.

Obama is also black. He remembers discussions of racial put downs in his home. He writes about other personal incidents in his two best-selling books. And Obama describes how he read stories of racial discrimination against black people. Though not in Martin Luther King Jr.'s movement, Obama was aware of its challenges, goals, and setbacks.

Obama also comes from an immigrant background. His father was from Kenya and immigrated to the U.S. to get a famous education. Father Obama did not come to America to find the American dream—to get married, have children, and seek permanent residence and naturalized citizenship. Rather, Mr. Obama saw the U.S. as a place to obtain the best resources and then return to his own home in Kenya. The consciousness and history of the father Obama were not rooted in the usual black American story. Rather, his heart and priority were at home in Kenya.

This contrasts with the standard script of most black Americans' story. That is to say, they come mainly from the west coast of Africa, and they were brought to the "New World" involuntarily in chains starting in 1619, four hundred years ago. Before European colonizers came to the continent, the usual African American story gives examples of how West Africa had empires with kings and queens and philosophers and advanced civilizations. In contrast, Obama is the son of a free father, a voluntary immigrant arriving at Harvard University in 1959 from the east coast of Africa.

In addition to being multiracial (that is, genetically and socialization-wise), Obama is also multicultural. He grew up in Hawaii: the state that shows the beauty and possibility of what all of the U.S. can become. While recognizing the justice issues of Hawaii's nationhood status is an ongoing struggle, Hawaii offers a different perspective about human community. Obama matured in this environment of Native Hawaiians, Japanese Hawaiians, and Chinese Hawaiians. Other groups live on the island, such as Pacific Islanders, whites, and blacks. To be in Hawaii is to be in an environment of many people, foods, and languages. Hawaii can suggest the possibility of multicultural tolerance and global communities settling among Native Hawaiians.

In contrast, Jeremiah A. Wright Jr. comes from inner-city Philadelphia and from a black family that traces parts of its roots back to Virginia and the slavery era. And Wright is a third-generation black preacher.

Wright's world was intensely racialized by the awareness of Africa's contributions to all humanity, his slavery history, northern racial discrimination, and the segregation he experienced when he went South for his BA degree. At the same time, he grew up in a loving household and city where blacks told folktales; remembered the heroics of enslaved blacks; swayed with jazz rhythms, doo-wop, and R & B; and played the dozens on ghetto street corners. Wright knew about other great black achievements such as the Harlem Renaissance, A. Phillip Randolph's threat against Franklin Delano Roosevelt if the president didn't integrate the armed services, and Martin Luther King Jr. and Malcolm X.

Wright speaks about his biological white racial body when he describes how some southern white slave master raped an enslaved black woman and, out of this violent white-black intimacy comes Wright's own "white blood." This, however, does not erase his positive and favorable experiences he had with Philadelphia whites and Jews.

Wright came to Chicago and there dedicated his ministry to the extremely racially segregated South Side. Chicago is classic black America with its family-history links to the European slave trade on the African west coast, U.S. slavery, segregation, and the almost-herculean efforts that blacks see themselves using to overcome the odds against them. Wright is part of and enjoys this standard story. Here black folk celebrate, worship in, and relax in the cultural safety of other black people. At the same time, this black American story remembers the history of the Tuskegee syphilis experiment that the U.S. government carried out on black men's bodies.

Wright comes out of a specific line of black preaching. His father was a big-name Baptist preacher in Philadelphia, and his father was a son of a Baptist preacher. Thus Jeremiah Wright Jr. symbolizes three generations of the prophetic wing of the black church, one where Christianity is empty rhetoric if not linked to social justice and occasional prophetic denunciation of the powerful. Similarly, Wright practices a form of black religious speech that combines the fullness of the body with the intellect. Indeed, black preaching is a verbal and bodily ritual of performance.

Wright and Obama—the preacher and the politician, race and multiculturalism—have different parental, geographic, historical, and personal experiences. Yet both agree on the Bible as being partial to the poor. Both agree on church function as organizing justice.

Wright is deeply rooted in a segregated black community and the importance of their voice and their obtaining resources for living. From that particularity he bridges into conversation and coalition with all of America. In contrast, Obama begins with a vision for all of America. From that perspective, blacks are simply one strand among many in a larger tradition about whites and blacks (as well as yellows, browns, and reds) being their brothers' and sisters' keepers.

One is a preacher rooted in service to a local church. The other is a politician moved to serve the larger nation. The preacher's prophetic vocation and the politician's universal leadership could have held together in one church building. Race and multiculturalism were connected in one Christian institution. But with the intense media scrutiny of Trinity United Church of Christ, an experiment of these two differences unified in faith and service to the poor could not remain in close relations in a presidential election year. And so the politician resigned his membership so both he and the church could no longer be distracted. However, in the long-term health of the nation, America needs both types of black male leaders at the table of civic discussions and citizens' democracy.

2

A New Black Heterosexual Male

Too many people within the African American community, church, and black theology believe that gender concerns only women. When the gender issue becomes the center of discussion, most black men, for example, become like corpses. Their tongues grow silent; their bodies drop to a limp posture; and their presence fades into a ghostlike absence. Gender, from their vantage point, relates only to black women. If this logic is true, they reason, then it would be another example of black male sexism to enter the conversation and dominate what is said and not said. The flipside of this belief is that African American men do not have a gender, which is obviously false. Black men have a male gender, so gender refers to both men and women.

Gender differs from sex. Sex speaks to human biology, the genitalia with which each person is born, while gender is defined and determined not by nature but by human culture. Usually human nurturing cannot change sex. But gender construction remains a socialization process influenced by child-rearing and parenting models, peer pressure and positive examples, movies and other media, educational institutions and training organizations, and biblical interpretation and faith communities. Human beings make other human beings into specific male and female genders.

Restated, gender represents both a cultural category and a dynamic process of socialization. Culture includes every aspect of a person's way of believing, thinking, judging, saying, and doing in the world. Culture, moreover, indicates a communal existence. There are no cultures of individuals, only cultures of people, groups, and communities. As a result, we identify an individual based on his or her relation to and interaction with a group. Group culture contains certain rituals and myths that glue the culture together and help to distinguish one type of culture from another. Furthermore, culture always carries a specific language spoken by a community.

As it is a product of socialization, gender is not formed overnight, nor is it ever a completely finished product. As a vibrant creation, gender follows the ongoing formation of a culture. Cultures of groups do not remain static. In the process of cultures changing themselves continually, cultures also impact the definition of gender. Consequently, gender becomes a liquid category. It is solid like ice and liquid like water; and it evaporates like mist. Furthermore, socialization tells us that there exists no absolute identification of gender. From this perspective, there are no right or wrong definitions of gender because gender results from how each society socializes people into gender roles.

For black theology of liberation, the key to whatever gender relationships take place in a community is not the description of the genders but the presence or absence of liberation, the ethics of equality, and mutual sharing. In other words, when babies are born, they can become any gender that society socializes them to be. If the privileges that come along with being male rather than female are created by human beings (who go against the spirit of divine liberation), then human beings (who work with the spirit to practice equality) can bring about social change to remove these privileges from the male gender.

Human societies use the dynamic process of socialization to produce a desired gender. The family remains the basic unit for modeling male and female genders. Other factors of influence are schools, sports, visual and audio entertainment, sex roles, jobs and professions, churches and other faith institutions, news media, languages, myths, rituals, laws, and race. Especially within the United States of America, the monopoly capitalist system sets the broader context for all definitions and formations of gender. This political economic structure maintains a bottom-line culture of absolute profit making at the expense of the majority of the people. The root of the profit culture is private ownership of capital and wealth by a small, elite group of families headed by men.

Even more specifically, capitalist democracy means placing a minority of males of a certain race in power positions and as owners of wealth and capital. Immediately we notice a hierarchy of gender as well as class and race. This monopoly capitalist democracy hierarchy of the minority over the majority thrives on seeing another human being as someone to be used and dominated for profit and the accumulation of more wealth. From the arrival of the first permanent English-speaking European colonies in Jamestown, Virginia, in 1607, to the constitutional convention in Philadelphia, Pennsylvania, in 1787, every foundation of the United States has been based on male superiority. This male-gender hierarchy has become so ingrained in the hearts and minds of both women and men that no one even questions the pervasive reality of power positions and wealth ownership belonging to a minority U.S. population—men of a certain racial grouping. From 1607 to the twenty-first century, voting and laws have not dislodged this entrenched monopoly capitalist, democratic minority of white men.

In the larger process of male socialization, black men experience a double male-gender reality, and both sides of this reality are negative. On one hand, the broader culture of white society defines and portrays black men as subordinate to white men. African American men are socialized to conform to the male gender but as men who are subordinate to the racial supremacy of another male gender. On the other hand, within the African American community, black men are socialized to adopt the standard definition of the male gender that is established and defined by the larger white male culture. As a result, too many black men strive toward and enjoy male privileges over black women and children within the African American family and community. When black men adopt and implement the patriarchy of the wider white male culture, they can act out a very sinful and potentially deadly force on those around them. Specifically, too often African American men store up both their frustrations and anger against white men with power and then release these two demons onto the women, children, and other black men within their own families and communities.

To sum up, the negative white male culture establishes the standard for what it means to be a black man, and too many African American men follow this harmful standard. But to imitate this unethical goal from outside of the black community and family means accepting one's black manhood as subordinate to white manhood. At the same time, problems with white men of power and wealth lead too many black men to see their home or their community as their royal domain where they are king and everyone else serves as their subjects. Black men experience a state of victimization by white male superiority, and they simultaneously enjoy male privilege at home and in their neighborhoods.

A system of negative white male culture in the United States not only sets the standard for what is a male gender, but it creates and perpetuates stereotypes about the black male gender. Thus, African American men can never fully reach the standard set by white patriarchy because black men, although males, are not white. At the very same time that they experience this barrier blocking them from realizing the standard, they suffer from a barrage of sinful stereotypes. The visual and audio media in North America shows blacks as entertainers through the professions of sports (i.e., Michael Jordan), comedy (i.e., Eddie Murphy), and the military (i.e., Colin Powell).

Black men, in the broader culture, are portrayed as being more physical, more powerful, and stronger, meaning more sensuous and sexy. As the perfect sexual supermen, African American males are seen as connoisseurs of the sexual act, having the most endurance and physical equipment and possessing an identity motivated by a life in pursuit of the sexual act. Black men, in the logic of these myths, are more emotional, volatile, and unpredictable. Likewise, they lack intelligence and the values of reason, thoughtfulness, academic insight, and deliberate judgment. This false picture also suggests that African American males are untrustworthy in the areas of wealth and finance, while they have a natural gift for being criminals and engaging in illegal activity. They do not like to work or to work hard and are irresponsible. They are not leaders but followers. In these stereotypes, black males also abandon their children and depend on black women or on white people to support them.

African American men can do one of two things. They can accept this false understanding of the black male gender, or they can choose to create something new. If they accept the negative white male culture and practices of male gender and the stereotypes that go along with them, then they should honestly admit that they suffer as victims of a larger structure, but, at the same time, they should confess that they also are making conscious choices to carry out the harmful aspects of this structure. This conscious choice has devastating consequences on black women and children in particular. Basically, males who make this wrong decision opt for very harmful power-and-control strategy and tactics against African American women. These tactics include persuading black women that they should support the black man at all costs because he is a victim of white male oppression; intimidation, emotional abuse, and isolation of black women; denying or minimizing (or both) any wrongdoing but blaming the women; using children against women; using male privilege (acting like the king of the castle or making all decisions); and carrying out economic abuse, verbal threats, physical violence, or sexual violence (i.e., through direct physical force or nagging pursuit).

Refusing to opt for this harmful and abusive choice, African American men can start to reconstruct what it means to be a new heterosexual male. They can begin first by accepting the love of God that is in all black men. The root of all harmful attitudes and actions against black women and children comes from black men's lack of self-love. But self-love can come to reality only when men understand and feel a love that is greater than any one person. It is a transcendent love, a divine love, a love that grows from the collective body. In this sense, it is not an individual love, but a communal love that floods the very being of the individual as a gift of love proceeding from the community into the soul of the individual. Divine love found within black men matches a sacred love for and from the family and community. Ultimate love or God's love means that God loves black men in spite of the broken vessels that they are.

Such a love has profound implications for the ongoing struggle of African American people to achieve an inclusive and complete liberation and to practice freedom. The movement for liberation cannot be sustained through the inevitable ups and downs and forward and backward steps and the high successes as well as the stinging defeats unless black men love themselves. And the starting point is recognition and acceptance of God's unconditional love. Indeed, God's love gives the black man a sacred power that makes his loyalty not to any earthly demonic structures or individual authority figures but to something that transcends the boundaries of this world. Equipped with this love and power in one's feelings and one's intellect, in one's heart and one's head, African American men no longer will have to choose unhealthy and harmful options.

On the contrary, the struggle for liberation and the practice of freedom become one's vocation from God. This calling places all social relations, uncontrolled cravings, negative pulls of a weak black male ego, endless tasks, and incorrect focus on the individual self into perspective. Thus, self-love is not a self-centered practice or feeling where one's worldview and lifestyle become "I pursue money, profit and wealth, therefore I am." Nor does this love indicate a touchy-feely state of being in the world. It is love of self founded on divine love, which subordinates the lifestyle of the individual African American male to help liberation from negative personal and social structures and toward a practice of freedom defined by equality. Such a love brings a healthy life in the family, in the community, and among all humankind.

A spirituality of love from God acts as the foundation for the definition of the self. Spirituality, however, exists in the material, real, tangible world. A true heterosexual black male, full of God's love, takes a stand against a host of devious desires and damaging deeds. He speaks out against various discriminations pertaining to race, gender, class, sexual orientation, and ecological issues. The starting point and yardstick remain justice and freedom for all, beginning with the most oppressed communities in society and the poor. When he lives in the world with this type of talk and walk, he inevitably meets those who wish to maintain their privileges of race, class, gender, sexual orientation, and human cravings over all of God's creation. Therefore, when an African American man stands with the majority (the suffering and vulnerable) in contrast to the minority (the monopolist capitalist democracy for the few who hoard wealth and power), his very reason for living will be challenged. Those with absolute economic power will use different ways to attack the very idea of God's love for black men and, consequently, black men's divine-given self-love. But the more African American men withstand this trial and the more they feel good about themselves, the more likely there will be healthy black families and communities. Again, good feelings and healthy conditions come from participation in struggle for intentional self-development and collective transformation. Transformation requires work, work requires discipline, discipline requires sacrifice, sacrifice requires motivation from a higher calling, and a calling requires a recognition of being loved, and being loved empowers one to love oneself and thereby to free others from the external structures and internal demons in their lives.

For Christians, Jesus stands for this liberation love. God's work in and through Jesus did not depend on and had nothing to do with the fact that Jesus was a man biologically. However, the way Jesus developed his male gender gives us a model for the construction of today's new black heterosexual male. Because Jesus was so caught up in the mission of the sacred spirit who had anointed him to be with the poor on the divine-human journey to practice freedom, he loved himself enough based on this spiritual vocation. This spirituality of love led to a self-love that energized Jesus's compassion for the outcasts around him. The most striking example is revealed in how Jesus talked to, spent time with, listened to, answered the questions of, healed, and empowered women to become their full selves. He accepted both male and female disciples. He appointed women as well as men to carry out the work of justice from God. Women became the first preachers to proclaim the liberation revelation of Jesus as the risen Christ. Jesus ordained them to carry forth the good news that death caused by a political crucifixion no longer had the final word. In fact, he broke the status quo boundaries around and oppressive definitions of what it meant to be both male and female. Any black male who believes and acts as if any black female is secondary, by definition, does the work of the antichrist. He goes against the entire birth, life, ministry, and tradition of Jesus the Anointed One. For the followers of Christianity, he has strayed, intentionally or unintentionally, from the path of life.

A theological reconstruction of the black male consists not only of the love of God and the life of Jesus, but also of an acceptance that God is black for African American males. To be made in the image of God compels black males to make a leap into the blackness of God's essence for them. To worship and surrender total allegiance to something or someone alien to African American males is slow self-destruction and internal spiritual death. A black God affirms every physical characteristic of what the United States calls black. And God says it is good. This knowledge brings about radical results precisely because a spiritual vision, value, and vocation overcomes all the negative stereotypes forced on and propagated against black males. God, as a spirit of equality, reveals in the biological and physical characteristics of African American males. Such a claim can cause a disruption in the minds of men.

Specifically, for too long many black males have been on their knees praying to an old white man with gray hair. On the theological level, this is nonsense since black citizens represent the image of God. Therefore, theologically, God by necessity is black if black people are images of God. And on the psychological and emotional level, praying to a white male god has meant, in the context of North America, too many black people willingly giving their complete selves to the very same image of the system and structure of the supremacy of whites over blacks. This old, gray-haired, white god has been one of the deepest causes for black self-hatred. In this sinful faith of self-hatred, black men can be themselves only by first becoming white. However, neither whites nor blacks are divine in and of themselves. God is black for African American males due to the divine compassion for those on the bottom of society's structure. Again, God's spirit is a spirit of liberation, and it chooses to reveal itself as black to be with the "little ones" of this earth. When African American men go against their black culture, context, and characteristics, they oppose the God of their own human liberation.

Not only is God black, but God is both father God and mother God. First of all, the being of God is a spirit. Human speech simply gives various verbal symbols for this divine spirit of liberation and freedom. For example, Jesus, the spirit's decisive revelation for Christians, has various human symbols for divine power—the Savior, the Liberator, Son of God, Son of Man, Mary's Baby, Lily of the Valley, the Shepherd, the Alpha and the Omega, and so forth. Again, human beings receive the spirit and attempt to name the revelation in the best way possible to explain the presence and power of God. The spirit cannot be contained within one human symbol. The human symbol or description called "father God" represents only one alternative. The male symbol for God—that is, father God—represents only one gender. Left by itself, that excludes 70 percent of the African American church and over 50 percent of the black community. We cannot limit the power and presence of God to one gender. God gave birth to all of humanity and all of creation. God watched over this creation and nurtured it, protected it, taught it, and gave and gives life to it. Therefore, God's spirit also appears in the human symbol of "mother God."

Theologically, we all are made in God's image; consequently black women reflect the female gender of God—mother God. When black men continue to pray to father God only, they are perpetuating and protecting African American men's privileges and expectations of automatic entitlement. Similarly, they continue to subordinate black women and deny the divine reality in their ebony sisters. Men—unfortunately with the help of some women—have established gender hierarchy with a patriarchal god who says he has all power. But this power is limited to one gender. Likewise, this power is limited to hierarchy and not equality. A limited divinity is not God, but the creation of black men who benefit from assuming that African American women are secondary creations of God. A further example of this point is seen with the clear contrast in the emphasis on God's blackness or Africanness on the part of some black men. Why do black men not fight as hard for the female gender of God as they struggle for God's black and African dimensions?

An African dimension does occupy a prominent position in the reconstruction of the new black male. African Americans have a mixed background and identity. Centuries have made them essential to what has become the space and time called the United States of America. Simultaneously, however, a black man recognizes and develops the legacy of his African ancestry. The African part of the black male is the very difference that distinguishes his divine identity. In the belief structures of West African peoples—from whom the majority of present-day black Americans are descended—sacred and secular operate together. Otherwise, God would be impotent and missing from some aspect of God's reality. If black men are to enjoy a full life, then they respond to a calling that covers all aspects of everyday practices in the United States. Faith stretches beyond a ritual on Sunday or a private prayer. The presence of faith helps the underdogs of society to risk standing up against their earthly oppressors and live as healed and whole beings in the private, public, personal, and political spheres. The God of liberation teaches the new black male to be a man wherever he breathes.

Furthermore, the West African tradition gives a black man a sense of respect based on how well he participates with, takes care of, and shares in the African American family. This tradition goes against the idea of the absent, authoritative, nonvulnerable, domineering North American male, who expects privileges simply because of his biological makeup and a negative affirmative action based simply on his male gender. The West African influence, moreover, focuses a black man on the community's well-being. "I am because we are," and "Without community, one is a subhuman animal" become the standard of the African American male's lifestyle. The new black male opposes me-first and profit-first capitalist individualism at the expense of the collective. Such a deadly practice and demonic religion puts one race or gender or class or sexual orientation "first" above others.

Planting Seeds

Since, 1998, I have been part of a gathering of men that intentionally sees itself as planting a "mustard seed" for eventual clarity on how to talk through and walk into what it means to be a new heterosexual black male. We consist of black Christian, heterosexual males, most of whom are married to or in relationships with African American women; and we are all members of black churches. Self-described as a men's house group, we meet twice a month on Saturdays at 7:00 a.m. For us, with at least fourteen members, this space and time provide the conditions for a sacred, complete perspective on life. We participate in prayer and Bible study, and read liberation materials and theories from a host of disciplines and subject matters. We have read black theology and womanist theology writings; we have spent time covering literature on the plight of and possibilities for the black male in America. We have learned about meditation and spiritual formation. We also look at documentary videos from the Reverend Adam Clayton Powell Jr., Martin Luther King Jr., Toni Morrison, Paul Robeson, John Coltrane, Fred Hampton, and various black preachers and black churches. Moreover, we spend quite some time discussing our duties to our wives, children, and grandchildren.

Our sharing on political, cultural, economic, local, national, and international events helps us to think individually about the joys (praise reports) and pains (prayer concerns) of each man in the room. In these sacred moments, tears have been shed and discussions have taken place about working with poor black folk and protesting some injustices in the African American community. An ongoing focus is how to become strong black Christian males who can accept the love of God and love of the self and work with black women to improve the African American family and community. However, the final goal is to participate in the well-being of the least in every society of the world. Some of the men involve themselves in areas of direct political work, economic development, or grooming a new generation of young black men through rites-of-passage programs. We have experienced heated debates on African American parenting and on the ups and downs of Wall Street. Self-criticism has become a part of the program, especially when we discuss how we participate in the liberation of poor blacks; this shows in the areas of providing jobs, increasing black health, writing on behalf of the voiceless, proclaiming the gospel of good news and justice for the oppressed, educating others, and creating right relationships in other ongoing projects.

From the perspective of black theology, the question of the creation of a new heterosexual black male gender flows like a weaving process. It never progresses in a straight line. Like all scientific discoveries, quality relationships, and the implementation of the finest visions, becoming something new is a many-layered process. Sometimes the newness reveals itself as bright as the morning sun or as clear as the brilliance of a black summer night. Other times the struggle falters and goes backward, gripped in the old hand of male privilege. But the foundation of this crucial effort is an openness to what black theology claims so adamantly: that God loves the poor and those who work on justice for the least in society. That is the purpose for the revelation of Jesus the Anointed One on earth. Male chauvinism (the attitude of superiority), male privileges (the practice of this attitude), and patriarchy (the system that exists in spite of how nice individual men are) go against every thing that God, Jesus, and West African ancestors have called black men to think, be, say, and do. The good news is that African American men will be fully human when black women achieve their full humanity. I am because we are. And we are part of a faith and a tradition that says, "God may not come when you call God, but God is always right on time."

3

Poor Brother, Rich Brother: Faith, Family, and Education

Their litany is lethal, if not genocidal: Twenty-five percent of African American males between the ages of twenty and twenty-nine are either on parole, incarcerated, or under some other control of the criminal justice system. The United States government imprisons African American males at a rate four times greater than apartheid South Africa jailed its black male population. Forty percent of black males who drop out of school cannot find employment; overall unemployment among black youth in some areas stands at 70 percent. The black community makes up roughly 12 percent of the U.S. population but, with black males belonging to a significant portion, represents over 44 percent of drug possession arrests and over 27 percent of the reported AIDS cases. Up to 70 percent of black homes have no fathers present. Furthermore, murder is the number-one cause of death among African American males between the ages of fifteen and thirty-four.[1]

In a different vein, black middle-income and professional men face their own problems of success. They are only 4 percent of all undergraduate faculty. In 1976, blacks received 6.6 percent of all MA degrees; in 1989, 4.9 percent. In the same year, blacks earned 4.3 percent of all professional degrees; in 1989, 4.4 percent. In 1979, 1,056 doctorates were conferred on African Americans; in 1989, only 811.[2] Black businessmen cannot get needed loans regardless of their credit rating. In addition, white affluent suburbia has forced back middle-income families into segregated black "ghetto" spots. And, with unforgettable reminders, the perpetual glass

---

1. These statistics come from mainstream publications during this article's time period.

2. These statistics come from mainstream publications during that time period.

ceiling remains a relentless symbol of what black professional men read in the statistics and what they experience in their gut. Regardless of their qualifications, black professionals know that white junior colleagues with poorer credentials may someday become their bosses.[3]

Clearly, the various structures of white racist encounters of black poor and middle-income males mean at least two things. First, both groups suffer from a system of racial and cultural discrimination. No matter what one's station in life, if you are a black man in North America, racism is common place like the nation's taste for apple pie. For example, black middle-income males wearing four-thousand-dollar Armani suits have been left standing on the curbsides in frustration because taxicabs refused to pick them up. Furthermore, many whites quickly close elevators on black men who are corporate executives in the very same buildings housing these black executives. And white women, in broad daylight, are oftentimes just as likely to cross a street and clutch their pocketbooks whether they are facing an oncoming middle-income or poor black man. In a word, a pervasive set of codes and attitudes regarding black males glue together the total African American experience, regardless of background.

Second, we can find big gaps in the degree of racial oppression between these two occupants of different economic classes. Black poor underclass or working-class men do not even have the opportunity to face housing discrimination or the possible runaround in attempts to buy vacation homes in the Caribbean, Hawaii, or Martha's Vineyard. Likewise, they cannot complain about the shabby (racist?) service that waiters and waitresses provide in a three-hundred-dollar-a-meal restaurant. For the poor, discussion about whether to live among black citizens or in Westchester County, New York, or Atherton, California, is a foreign language. More than likely, they will not focus on the debate over whether to send their children (or go themselves) to historically black colleges or to one of the eight elite Ivy League universities. They will not face the luxury of purchasing a Mercedes, a Jaguar, a BMW, a Land Rover, or an expensive Japanese top-of-the-line car for comfort and status. Thus, black men (and, indeed, the entire African American community) experience a "rich brother–poor brother" problem. But what concerns us is not so much the controversy over the primacy of white racism or economic class as the main evil facing black men. Clearly, the connection of these two demonic faces (among others) has to be a central

---

3. For issues facing African American males, see Kenneth Meeks, *Driving While Black: Highways, Shopping Malls, Taxicabs, Sidewalks: How to Fight Back If You Are a Victim of Racial Profiling* (New York: Broadway Books, 2000); and Manning Marable, ed., *Dispatches from the Ebony Tower: Intellectuals Confront the African American Experience* (New York: Columbia University Press, 2000).

part of any faith analysis or solution. What concerns us here are the value judgments and lifestyles that could impact whatever debates and practical solutions dealing with the growing gap between poor and rich black males. Coming from the side of the black male professional sector, I think part of the foundation for bridging the gap lies in the preaching and practice of faith, family, education, and political culture.

Above all, the African American Christian church has been the first advocate and leader of what it means to have faith in the black community in general. More specifically, the black church, from slavery until today, remains the main institution for gathering and training black men for leadership and accountability to the entire African American community. This intergenerational training has taken place regardless of one's class or stature. It planted a spiritual awareness, which laid the groundwork for the ethical practice of better-off males helping those with less economic and political power.

Furthermore, the black church has provided a haven for black men who suffer the daily humiliations and destructive macho images of a predominantly white society. The church, in other words, has offered a refuge, has encouraged family responsibility, and has allowed black men to experience their own feelings. One of the few public places where African American males can cry and also be affirmed about their strong place in the family is the black church. Any bridging of the poor brother–rich brother divide has to either start with the church or eventually include black religious institutions of all denominations and faith persuasions at the hub of its activities.

Closely aligned with the church is the importance and decisive role of the black family in leading the rebuilding of the relationships between rich and poor black males. Since the original days in Africa and, more negatively, since the forced removal of the fathers and brothers from the enslaved family, African Americans have always believed that the absence of a male figure in the nuclear family household does not eliminate the strength of male role models throughout the broader communal ties.

Put differently, the rich brothers have to present themselves and their vocations as instances of God's possibilities for the have-nots of African American families, in both blood and nonblood ties. Many times, poor black brothers have to react violently and uselessly to the damning negatives imposed by the larger white society as a way of asserting their "manhood" since many of the images and networks the poor have are harmful black role models of a "bad nigger."

A "bad nigger" is antitraditional black family, a baby maker without responsibility, a gunslinger and a cool dresser, whose substance is the cadence of his rap and hip in his hop. Therefore, following "each one teach one" and "lift as we climb," those black professional or middle-income black males who have or are on the way to "making it" cannot forget how they got over.

In addition to the church, some black male mentor, father, grandfather, businessman, doctor, teacher, scoutmaster, coach, principal, politician, old man across the street, or barber talked to young black men and showed them what was possible. Indeed, it was this extended family black male that inspired many young black men to move to higher levels of self-achievement and simultaneously maintain a sense of accountability toward the larger black community. As these younger men went out into the world, these older African American men always reminded the youth that they not only represented themselves in what they did, but their conduct, worth, and achievements also reflected back on the black family and community. All "rich brothers," then, have to position themselves, at some level, so that brothers faced with literal life-and-death issues can know what family means. Middle-income African American men share a related responsibility to black male children in both their nuclear and extended families.

Likewise, education complements the foundational values of church and family. Those better-off black males who recognize and affirm the worth of education must give knowledge to poor brothers who do not. There has always been a group of black males in their communities who did not believe that it was a "sissy thing" to study, attend classes, and do homework. To be "down" with what is happening meant being up on the books. But unfortunately today there stubbornly persists a strong culture to harass African American male youth who take educational studies seriously. Such a backward tendency can be replaced with a positive connection between African American "manhood" and the life of the mind. How can an enriched black self-identity and African-centricity take place if poor brothers cannot even read? A powerful intracommunity alliance needs to redirect the profound intellectual energy found in the "street" black males' ability to rap and "play the dozens." They need to know that their important street wisdom is the same mind power that can be used for the more traditional creative learning. That new understanding will happen when they grasp the power of education for both self-esteem and social transformation.

Education can open up for the poor brother not only increased preparedness for jobs but also a whole new horizon concerning what other people of color around the world are doing and what are the historical traditions of the black life in this country. Consequently, education is practical. It uses solidarity and subversive preparation against a destructive status quo. Black professional males need to share a fuller meaning of understanding with those who have "turned off" to public schools.

Finally, let us consider the value of black political culture. A middle-income African American and poor male relationship should base itself primarily on the positive cultural resources within the African American community. By "culture," I mean everything and anything that black people possess that can halt the genocide of the African American male population in North America. Culture is a lifestyle; it is both written and oral, conscious and unconscious. It is how one practices one's daily affairs, how one sleeps, eats, works, and interacts with others. Black culture includes the total connection as well as a specific self-identity. But the rallying of an internal black culture has important implications insofar as it is also political. By "politics," I mean remaking a larger power system currently based on individualism and the monopolistic hoarding of God's gifts by roughly two hundred megarich white American families.

For instance, in the last twelve months of his life, Martin Luther King Jr. processed and grasped this point when he proclaimed: "We must recognize that if we are to gain our God-given rights now, principalities and powers must be confronted and they must be changed."[4] For the "rich brother" with access to monies, networks, electoral politics, media, and more, there is a need to keep in focus the larger societal picture. Ultimately, the plight of the poor brother depends partly on the democratization of the major economic resources in North America. Restated, it depends partially on changing the faceless power brokers' club (i.e., the old boys' network). Those black brothers who have "made it" should not stop now. A society that allowed the rich brother to sneak through has to give way to a democratic one that prioritizes and privileges the life of the poor brother.

In the final analysis, the quality of the life and spiritual peace of the middle-income black males rests on the predicament and prospects of the poor brothers.

I do not suggest that guilt will energize the rich brother to search for ways to implement faith, family, education, and political culture as adequate value judgments and lifestyles. Guilt can only lead to condescension. On the contrary, programs to relate to poor and working-class black males should come from middle-income blacks because the latter's lives are also at stake. At one level, the rich brother's own humanity is threatened and lost as long as the poor brother suffers. To be human, in the African and African American tradition, means one is in community. Broken humanity somewhere affects humanity everywhere.

---

4. Quoted in David Garrow, *Bearing the Cross: Martin Luther King, Jr. and the Southern Christian Leadership Conference* (New York: Vintage, 1988), 581.

On another level, ethics dictates that it is the right thing to do. This belief lives deep within African American culture. Sometimes one calls it "what goes around comes around," or "you reap what you sow" or "God don't like ugly." In any case, it believes in a faith in the inevitability of nature's laws to move toward justice for the weak. On a third level, Christian, African American brothers have the added responsibility and joy of doing God's work for those without voices who are in pain. For when Christ calls one to accountability, rich and poor brothers should hope to hear Christ's words: "For I was hungry and you gave me food, I was thirsty and you gave me drink, I was a stranger and you welcomed me, I was sick and you visited me, I was in prison and you came to me . . . Truly, I say to you, as you did it to one of the least of these, my brothers, you did it to me" (Matt 25:31–46, ESV).[5]

---

5. From the ESV® Bible (The Holy Bible, English Standard Version®), copyright © 2001 by Crossway, a publishing ministry of Good News Publishers. Used by permission. All rights reserved.

4

The Construction of the Black Male Body: Eroticism and Religion

Like the pounding blows of a steam hammer, devastating images of the African American male body repeatedly hit the United States public's psychic during the end of the 1990s. Recurring themes of sexual lust akin to religious fervor acted as primary planks in this construction of what it means to be a black man in America. Yet the stereotypical blueprinting of the African American male identity actually began to intensify at the close of the 1980s, specifically in the 1988 presidential campaign. Indeed, we will see that the American black male body, individual and corporate, is defined by eroticism and religion.[1]

Triangle of Desire

The 1988 presidential elections pitted the Republican George Bush (the elder) against the Democrat Michael Dukakis. Hoping to guarantee a victory in the fall elections, Bush carried out a tried-and-true formula from the U.S. culture and psychology. In a vicious attack media advertisement that proved quite successful, Bush drew heavily on then–Massachusetts Governor Dukakis's apparent record of being soft on crime. The state of Massachusetts under the governor's leadership had released African American Willie Horton, who, during his furlough, was convicted of raping a white woman. With this sensational case, Bush launched a national crusade to discredit Dukakis as a wimp regarding law and order. The image of Bush, the white

---

1. For an insightful thesis on the global black body, refer to Radhika Mohanram, *Black Body: Women, Colonialism, and Space* (Minneapolis: University of Minnesota Press, 1999), chaps. 1–2.

patriarch, defending the sacredness and purity of the innocent, American white female citizen from the rapacious copulating appetite of the out-of-control, black brute criminal saturated the airwaves. If not the decisive nail in the proverbial coffin of Dukakis's failed bid for the White House, this compelling false story of sex, sacredness, and race at least added to Bush's victory in November.[2]

The following year, a pregnant white Bostonian female, Carol Stuart, died from a gunshot blast. Her baby died also after a Caesarean section. White male Charles Stuart, the husband, claimed that this double homicide as well as his gunshot wound had been inflicted by an overpowering black man. The state authorities arrested at least three African American men in the process of discovering which black male in Massachusetts had committed such a heinous crime—the violation of innocent, white motherhood in America.

> Somewhere along the line the narrative failed and Charles Stuart committed suicide. Shortly thereafter, it became clear that he had concocted the ploy in order to kill his wife. Charles had rehearsed the events with his brother, who met the car shortly after the shooting to take away Carol's pocketbook, which also contained Charles' gun. At the end is the corpse of the white family as social construction, the feared result of violation from the "nigger rapist."[3]

These two sensationalized strategies of Bush and Stuart symbolized an ongoing U.S. legacy of the original American drama: white male and black male protagonists moving through scenes of violence of the black sexual body, religious-like obligation to defend the white female body, and intervention of the white male body, all impacted by the erotic. "A common structure, a triangle of desire, unites these cases on a paradigmatic level with the death of Emmet Till. Although each is a variation, the triangle positions black men and white men as adversaries in a contest over the body of women."[4]

---

2. See Robert E. Hood's *Begrimed and Black: Christian Traditions on Blacks and Blackness* (Minneapolis: Fortress, 1994), xi.

3. George P. Cunningham, "Body Politics: Race, Gender, and the Captive Body," in Marcellus Blount and George P. Cunningham, eds., *Representing Black Men* (New York: Routledge, 1996), 148.

4. Ibid., 134–35. Emmet Till, a fourteen-year-old black boy from Chicago visiting relatives in the Delta of Mississippi, was lynched in 1955 by two local white men because they stated explicitly they needed to protect southern white womanhood from black male sexual predators. Examine Stephen J. Whitfield, *A Death in the Delta: The Story of Emmet Till* (New York: Free Press, 1988); and *Awakenings (1954–1956)*, episode

Threshold of the Twenty-First Century

The 1990s showed the triangular process with even more force, often clouded over with suggestions of erotic pleasure at the expense of black bodies. For instance, after falsely arresting him, New York City police raped Abner Louima, a black man, by driving the handle of a toilet plunger up his anus. And in what could be considered an ecstatic climax of orgiastic violence, New York City police executed Amodou Diallo, a black man, with nineteen shots because they feared that this dark male body threatened their safety. (Diallo was actually reaching for his wallet.) The Federal Bureau of Investigation captured on tape District of Columbia mayor Marion Barry in a hotel with nonprescription drugs and a woman who was not his wife. The surveillance video suggested that the mayor planned to move in sexually on the woman after consuming the illegal substance. Michael Jackson experienced strip-searching and examination of his pubic hair by state authorities who implied that he had sexually molested a child. A group of white male citizens of Texas lynched James Byrd Jr., a black man, by dragging his body from the back of a moving vehicle through the street. Byrd lost his penis in the ordeal. The U.S. Senate's confirmation hearings of Clarence Thomas to the United States Supreme Court had white men judging the fate of a black man in the midst of sexual-predator accusations and high-tech lynching charges. (And who will ever forget the television framing of direct shots of Judge Thomas with a white wife on one side and a white male patron senator on the other.)[5] Rap star Tupac Shakur was accused of participating in a gang rape of a female.[6] A jury acquitted O. J. Simpson of murdering blond, blue-eyed Nicole Simpson while doubts persisted about his guilt and prior sexual and emotional domestic violence complaints.[7] Los Angeles police officers repeatedly dealt near-lethal blows to Rodney King's black body because they sensed he might overpower them with brute (erotic?) strength. (King had

---

1 of *Eyes on the Prize: America's Civil Rights Years 1954–1965*, produced by Mark Samels. The series is a production of Blackside Inc.; this episode was produced and directed by Judith Vecchione.

5. See an excellent analysis of the implications of the Thomas–Hill hearings in Marcia Y. Riggs's *Plenty Good Room: Women versus Male Power in the Black Church* (Cleveland: Pilgrim, 2003), 54–55.

6. Devon W. Carbado, "The Construction of O. J. Simpson as a Racial Victim," in Devon W. Carbado, ed., *Black Men on Race, Gender, and Sexuality* (New York: New York University Press, 1999), 159.

7. Ibid., 172. Toni Morrison deepens this conversation in her edited work, *Race-ing Justice, En-gendering Power: Essays on Anita Hill, Clarence Thomas, and the Construction of Social Reality* (New York: Pantheon, 1992).

two prior arrests for domestic abuse.)[8] In fact, one of the terrorist-like officers referred to King as "Gorillas in the Midst." And the courts convicted heavyweight boxing champion Mike Tyson of date rape and two counts of "deviant sexual conduct."[9]

Despite diverse instances and differing scenarios in the above stories, what we want to say is that the "triangle of desire" serves as the overarching backdrop for black men's forced American identity in U.S. culture and mentality. Moreover, the black-white males on white female shows the mix of eroticism and religion in the construction of the black male body. The United States' obsession with eroticism of the black body identity is akin to if not actually a religion, revealed in Christianity and the wider U.S. culture.[10]

A Sexualized Beast Body

Conceptually, the black male body has been created from several sources. The Frenchman René Descartes's theoretical reflections on the mind and body separation helped lay the seeds for and, thereby, influenced greatly the eighteenth-century European Enlightenment's understanding of a material and immaterial split in what it means to be a human being. In a word, the mind, symbolized by whites in Europe, looked for higher goals in the human situation, while the body, represented by blacks and other darker peoples of the globe, longed for expressions of lust. The body's traits mean "passion, biology, the inside, otherness, inertness, unchanging, statis, matter—a more primitive way of being. To the mind is attributed reason, the self, the same, action, movement and intelligence, a more developed way of being or *not* being."[11] In Descartes's *Discourse On Method* (1637, and further elaborated on in his *Meditations* 1641), the mind is pure thought, the body mere materiality. The mind can affect the body. The body can only be acted upon by the mind. In this sense, the body becomes an object and a mechanical instrument—a machine.[12] Particularly for black people, in this

---

8. Carbado, "Construction of O. J. Simpson as a Racial Victim,"159.

9. Examine Michael Awkward's "'You're Turning Me On': The Boxer, the Beauty Queen, and the Rituals of Gender," in Carbado, ed., *Black Men on Race, Gender, and Sexuality*, 129.

10. On the notion of American civic or civil religion Leroy S. Rouner offers a compelling analysis. For my purposes, I would add race-wealth-gender to his discussion. Compare Leroy S. Rouner, "What Is an American?" in *The Key Reporter/The American Scholar* (www.pbk.org/pubs/keyreporter/spring99/rounder.htm/).

11. Mohanram, *Black Body: Women, Colonialism, and Space*, 199.

12. Observe Dalia Judovitz's *The Culture of the Body: Genealogies of Modernity*, The Body, in Theory (Ann Arbor: University of Michigan Press, 2001), 68–69.

anthropological model black body comes from external factors and lacks power to think, decide, impact history, or forge a spirituality on its own. The black body is deficient by nature and creation. The white mind is pure intellect, decision making, or a proactive anthropology. The black body gives into fate; the white mind chooses freedom.[13] The white mind practices rational, calm deliberation. The black male body, in particular, thrives on raw animal eroticism.

Descartes's structures of thought have dangerous implications for African American Christians. Despite the sensuousness of play found in black church worship, most black Christians attempt at all costs to drive the funkiness of the black body out of that building. Rarely is the erotic mentioned, and in instances of sex talk it becomes prohibition: don't have sex before marriage, don't cheat on one's wife, don't have homosexual sex, don't let sex be your driving force in life, don't look at women's bodies, God sees what you're doing in the bedroom, and so forth.

> We continue to live in Cartesian captivity: the mind-body split thought up by philosopher Descartes flourishes in black theologies of sexuality. Except it is translated as the split between body and soul. Black Christians have taken sexual refuge in the sort of rigid segregation they sought to escape in the social realm—the body and soul in worship are kept one place, the body and soul in heat are kept somewhere else.[14]

The irony is African American Christians have opposed white Christian racists on grounds that they continue to pit a gospel of spiritual liberation against a gospel of material freedom for black citizens. For example, African American believers oppose white supremacists for telling blacks to have faith in a theology of "you can have the world; just give me Jesus" while, in the really real world, when blacks turn toward heaven, whites control earth. Yet, black Christians then unite with the same theological thought structures about the body–soul split. Conceptually, the separation between body and soul or body and mind persistently preached in too many black churches implies double trouble for black believers.

First, the church fails to create a positive theology of eroticism for the black body (especially the male identity), which helps to drive many

---

13. See Lewis R. Gordon, *Bad Faith and Antiblack Racism* (Amherst, NY: Humanity Books, 1999), 101.

14. Michael Eric Dyson, "When You Divide Body and Soul, Problems Multiply: The Church and Sex," in *Traps: African American Men on Gender and Sexuality*, ed. Rudolph P. Byrd and Beverly Guy-Sheftall (Bloomington: Indiana University Press, 2001), 316–17.

black men away from Christian institutions. Second, the idea of the split perpetuates further the dangerous myth that a theology separating mind and body reinforces religious beliefs that black people are "body" people. They desire indecent tastes, deviant sex, and lustful libido. So, blacks who support this split are actually affirming theories about their own bestiality and perversions.

An additional conceptual piece in how religion and eroticism contribute to the making of the black male body is prudish theology. Such a religious way of thinking comes from two reactionary ways of believing—self-denial Puritanism and conservative Victorianism. To be pure means restricting the mind from thinking about body eroticism and, above all, a guilt whipping to prevent practicing such activities. And a Victorian upholds high culture and advanced civilization, both of which contrast radically with the sexual practices of the peasant masses.

> In sharp contrast to the heat of most black worship experiences, there emerged almost immediately in black churches a conservative theology of sexuality. In part, this theology reflected the traditional teachings of white Christianity. Out of moral necessity, however, black Christians exaggerated white Christianity's version of "p.c."—Puritan Correctness. Later, many black Christians adopted white Christianity's Victorian repression to rebut the myth of black sexuality being out of control.[15]

A theology of antagonistic dualism and a theology of prudishism in the areas of eroticism and religion justify the construction of the black male body. The material and immaterial separation arises from Descartes's narrow personal experiences. The Victorian belief is just a cover to hide too many white Christians' negative cultural rumors about blacks. The Puritan thrust comes from a European legacy and the biblical Paul.[16]

Finally the idea of the male Black as Beast glues the triangular connection of African American male body on (white) female body defended by white male (authority) body. This corrupt idea tries to convince us in various examples. But, perhaps in the popular imagination, an old television commercial of National Basketball Association star Patrick Ewing represents a most sensational pornographic picture. In this TV ad, Ewing, then

---

15. Ibid., 313.

16. Though Paul was not among Jesus's twelve disciples and never met Jesus on earth, Paul occupies much more of the Christian Scriptures than Jesus's words. Thus Paul's theology carries a great deal of weight for black Christians. Furthermore, Paul believed that Jesus's return to earth was rather imminent, and the main thing was to prepare one's soul for the second coming of the Redeemer. So Paul is not known for embracing a positive theology of the body.

with the New York Knicks, is seen crawling up New York City's Empire State Building, itself thrust into the heavens as a symbolic phallus. A blaring echo of King Kong movies is hammered into the viewers' conscious and subconscious mind. With dark skin, flaring nostrils, close-cropped hair, and broad lips, the prostituting portrayal of Ewing strikes a similar pose like the sexual bestiality of the Kong freak. In the King Kong movies one has an overpowering black gorilla from the wilds of Africa brought into civilized New York City; and of the eight- to ten-million inhabitants, he stalks a blond, blue-eyed white female to hold in the palm of his gigantic hand. Could a black male thing so big actually physically love a white woman without crushing and splitting her open? And, following the predominant American cultural Hollywood script, it is powerful white men who understand their sacred crusade to destroy this ugly, black man-monkey.[17]

Moreover, this religious-like fervor against the erotic black beast forces the most wicked acts of all American males onto the black man's body. It is "an established fact that our culture links manhood to terror and power and that black men are frequently imaged as the ultimate in hypermasculinity . . . The cops who beat Rodney King and the jury who acquitted King's assailants openly admitted that the size, shape, and color of his body automatically made him a threat to the officer's safety."[18] Somehow black men have become a main cathartic scapegoat for the evils committed by all males.

Benefits of Scapegoating

Scapegoating inevitably means a sustained and systematic elaboration of an ultimate lie—ultimate in the sense of life-and-death specific meaning. To maintain singular focus on African American males as the ultimate center of all American male perversion, one has to comprehensively dress up falsehood with the air of scientific objectivity. But such scientism or commonsense beliefs avoid the true idea of erotic insecurity of the dominant male community in the U.S. For it "is still true, alas, that to be an American Negro male is also to be a kind of walking phallic symbol: which means that one pays, in one's personality, for the sexual insecurities of others."[19]

17. For other constructions of the black male body in the U.S. popular culture, refer to Phillip Brain Harper, *Are We Not Men? Masculine Anxiety and the Problem of African-American Identity* (New York: Oxford University Press, 1996).

18. Robin D. G. Kelley, "Confessions of a Nice Negro, or Why I Shaved My Head," in *Speak My Name: Black Men on Masculinity and the American Dream*, ed. Don Belton (Boston: Beacon, 1995), 15.

19. James Baldwin, *Price of the Ticket: Collected Nonfiction 1948–1985* (New York: St. Martin's, 1985), 290.

The dominating culture puts insecurities on black bodies because of the historical American white tradition's simultaneous fear and fascination, dislike and desire begun in slavery. Yet the push-pull of apparent polar opposites hides a fundamental cornerstone of erotic phobia about the black other's potential force in contrast to a white legacy of self-perceived impotency. There is "probably no greater (no more misleading) body of sexual myths in the world today than those which have proliferated around the figure of the American Negro. This means that he is penalized for the guilty imagination of the white people who invest him with their hates and longings, and is the principal target of their sexual paranoia."[20]

Imaginative scapegoating, therefore, draws together a comprehensive blackening of the non-white in order to create a story based on common-sense metaphor and scientific image. Colorful metaphor conjures up a collection of complex caricatures—sexually aggressive, violent, animalistic. And vibrant image offers visual frames and memorable pictures—primitive brute, aggressive sensuality, superhuman genitalia. Is this eroticism (that is, the addiction of focusing on black male, perverse body) and religiosity (that is, an ultimate life-and-death fixation) in mainstream construction of the black body simply about penis-size envy and, thus the notorious need to protect white womanhood?[21]

Perhaps. But the triangle of desire (i.e., black male body–woman body–white male body) is, as indicated previously, what dominant white American male culture imagines and uses for definite self-serving goals. "With respect to rape, for example, and as the white feminist Andrea Dworkin has observed, white men often employ and invoke the image of the black male rapist to obscure, deny, or excuse their own participation in this crime."[22] As a result, part of the black man's burden is to carry a disproportionate load of the legacy of those white men's evil sexual acts against white and black women. To be a male rapist in America translates into being an African American male.

However, metaphor and image must have support from a more powerful institution in order to convince most citizens and have transcendent

---

20. Ibid., 273.

21. In his *Constructing the Black Masculine: Identity and Ideality in African American Men's Literature and Culture* (Durham, NC: Duke University Press, 2002), Maurice O. Wallace argues that "Black men come to embody the inverse picture necessary for the positive self-portrait of white identity." This picture is what he calls an "ideograph for the American propensity to see black men half-blindly as a blank/black page onto which the identity theme of American whiteness, with its distinguishing terrors and longings, imprints itself as onto a photographic negative" (32).

22. Ishmael Reed, "Buck Passing: The Media, Black Men, O. J., and the Million-Man March," in Carbado, ed., *Black Men on Race, Gender, and Sexuality*, 46.

longevity. Enter the state apparatus, which even today is still controlled by a minority of U.S. citizens: powerful white men in executive, judicial, and legislative branches. The U.S. state apparatus created the fear of black men raping white women. This idea is not spontaneous. "It does not come from the people, who knew better, who thought nothing of intermarriage until they were penalized for it: this idea comes from the architects of the American state." Similarly the state created and manipulates the idea of black bodies as labor commodities for monopoly capitalism. "The idea of black persons as property, for example, does not come from the mob. It is not a spontaneous idea."[23]

And the (white) state functions in collusion with, if not at the instructions of, the small minority of white families who monopolize the majority of the wealth in the U.S.[24] To provide free (under slavery) and cheap (until today) black labor for white profit and further accumulation of wealth, the state works with the wealthy to convince the American pubic that black citizens are sensuous commodities. Toward this end, the white republic treated black people as less than human and then justified the treatment by grooming the public's mind that blacks were, in fact, less than human.

For instance, the thirteen colonies' and the U.S. government's support of slavery; the three-fifths clause in the U.S. Constitution; the government's providing land for white citizens in the Western "frontier"; the federal administration's backing segregation into the 1960s; federal, state, and local officials providing financial policies favoring the wealthy with a negative impact on the poor, made up disproportionately of African Americans; the state's removal of black people from their land or housing to make way for wealthy developers; and the state's collaboration with the wealthy elite to divide and conquer blacks and other minority citizens[25]—all indicate that

---

23. Baldwin, *Price of the Ticket*, xix.

24. Regarding the white wealthy minority that control the U.S. and their impact on black America, refer to Robert L. Allen, *Black Awakening in Capitalist America: An Analytic History* (Garden City, NY: Doubleday, 1969); Manning Marable, *How Capitalism Underdeveloped Black America* (Boston: South End, 1983); David Rockefeller, *Memoirs* (New York: Random House, 2002); Nelson W. Aldrich Jr., *Old Money: The Mythology of America's Upper Class* (New York: Vintage, 1989); Michael Parenti, *Democracy for the Few*, 2nd ed. (New York: St. Martin's, 1977); G. William Domhoff, *Who Rules America Now?* (Englewood Cliffs, NJ: Prentice-Hall, 1983); Richard C. Edwards et al., eds., *The Capitalist System: A Radical Analysis of American Society* (Englewood Cliffs, NJ: Prentice-Hall, 1972); David N. Smith, *Who Rules the Universities?* (New York: Monthly Review Press, 1974); Frances Fox Piven and Richard A. Cloward, *The New Class War: Reagan's Attack on the Welfare State and Its Consequences* (New York: Pantheon, 1982); and Felix Greene, *The Enemy: What Every American Should Know about Imperialism* (New York: Vintage, 1971).

25. Review Derrick Bell, "Sexual Diversion: The Black Man/Black Woman Debate

the humanity of black citizens (and red, brown, yellow, and poor white citizens) represents a low priority in America. The subordination of African Americans "was not an act of God, it was not done by well-meaning people muddling into something which they didn't understand. It was a deliberate policy hammered into place in order to make money from black flesh."[26] Furthermore, one could argue persuasively today that the disproportionate numbers of strong black men in prison in the twenty-first century comes from a deliberate collaboration between monopoly capitalist-related prison industries and local, state, and federal governments. Someone is making billions of dollars from the incarcerated black labor of black male bodies.

Echoes of the Past

The religious concept of sexualized black beast body (cemented in a theology of antagonistic dualism and a theology of prudishism) did not fall from the sky. A historical tradition has designed it with white, European Christianity as a main architect. "The church officially reinforced this entanglement of aesthetics, carnality, and negativity of blackness at the fifth-century Council of Toledo."[27] White religious men decided that Satan was a monster with huge genitalia. Three centuries later, one finds a naked black devil painted in Europe. Given this history of their Christian European ancestors, it is not totally surprising that when European ethnic groups came to the U.S. and changed their identity into "white" people (against blacks),[28] white Christianity and the broader U.S. civic religion (that is, white monopolization as

---

in Context," in Carbado, ed., *Black Men on Race, Gender, and Sexuality*, 239.

26. Harlon L. Dalton, "AIDS in Blackface," in Carbado, ed., *Black Men on Race, Gender, and Sexuality*, 328–29.

27. See Robert E. Hood's *Begrimed and Black*, 89.

28. There exists a beginning but vibrant intellectual tradition on the study of how European ethnic and tribal groups became "white" once they left their ancestors' continent and came to the land of the Native Americans (e.g., now the United States of America). For instance, see Thomas K. Nakayama and Judith N. Martin, eds., *Whiteness: The Communication of Social Identity* (Thousand Oaks, CA: Sage, 1999); Joel Kovel *White Racism: A Psychohistory* (New York: Columbia University Press, 1984); Birgit Brander Rasmussen et al., eds., *The Making and Unmaking of Whiteness* (Durham, NC: Duke University Press, 2001); Richard Delgado and Jean Stefanici, eds., *Critical White Studies: Looking behind the Mirror* (Philadelphia: Temple University Press, 1997); Mike Hill, ed., *Whiteness: A Critical Reader* (New York: New York University Press, 1997); Matthew Frye Jacobson, *Whiteness of a Different Color: European Immigrants and the Alchemy of Race* (Cambridge: Harvard University Press, 1998); and Theodore W. Allen, *Racial Oppression and Social Control*, The Invention of the White Race 1 (London: Verso, 1994).

THE CONSTRUCTION OF THE BLACK MALE BODY: EROTICISM AND RELIGION   49

a god-complex) enslaved Africans and African Americans.[29] Indeed, white "anxiety about alleged erotic allure of blacks exploded in America as early as 1662, when the British colony of Virginia passed a law that forbade sexual relations between black male slaves and white women." The white male rulers of the Virginia colony quoted biblical examples as justification.[30]

During the British colonial (1607–1776) and U.S. slavery (1619–1865) periods, white Christians instituted the castration of the black male body for at least two reasons. One rationale asserted the necessity of subduing "spirited" black men accused of raping white women. Another suggested a form of freaky voyeurism among segments of the dominant white population. Castration, here, was "linked to carnal curiosity about the black male's phallus," a perversion going back to ancient Greek and Roman civilizations.[31]

The Reconstruction era (1865–1877) saw the relative success of former enslaved blacks moving into government, civic, and business areas—areas of exclusive monopoly for privileged white men. As a result, lynching of black men became the order of the day. White Christian terrorists orchestrated beatings and hangings in the black community. "The closer the black man got to the ballot box, one observer noted, the more he looked like a rapist."[32] Lynching during post-Reconstruction, Jim Crow America became as common as "mom's apple pie." On one Sunday afternoon (the day of Jesus Christ), April 23, 1899, over one thousand white citizens congregated and frolicked to see the lynching of black male, Sam Hose. Like the overwhelming amount of cases, no evidence was produced. After chaining Mr. Hose to a tree, "they cut off his ears, fingers, and genitals, and skinned his face. While some in the crowd plunged knives into the victim's flesh." Jubilant participants removed his liver and heart while others broke up his bones. The festive crowd of Christians fought over these precious souvenirs. Crucified on resurrection Sunday, Hose's dying body deteriorated near an adjacent sign declaring "We Must Protect Our Southern Women."[33]

Throughout the South and Midwest, lynching persisted well into the twentieth century. It turned into a religious ritual symbolized both by its Sunday occurrences and also by a sense of (white) ethical duty to practice an American pastime. White terrorists often held prayer services prior to hangings. Christian fathers and mothers brought their girls and boys along

29. See Dwight N. Hopkins, *Down, Up, and Over: Slave Religion and Black Theology* (Minneapolis: Fortress, 1999).

30. Hood, *Begrimed and Black*, x.

31. Ibid., 150–51.

32. Leon F. Witwack, "Hellhounds," in *Without Sanctuary: Lynching Photographs in America*, ed. James Allen et al. (Santa Fe, NM: Twin Palms, 2000), 30.

33. Ibid., 9–10.

with picnic baskets. Some charted trains to attend this affair of entertainment. Entrepreneurial white men made instant postcards on the spot with white citizens taking pictures beside black men's castrated bodies, and then having these scenes developed into postcards to send to friends and relatives. White bankers, lawyers, merchants, and landed gentry occupied front row seats.

Yet the accused African American man rarely had had sex with a white woman. As a true motivation, wealthy white men, backed by those who followed them, wanted accumulation of more wealth under capitalism. A leading (1916) South Carolina newspaper wrote: black property "ownership always makes the Negro more assertive, more independent, and the cracker can't stand it."[34]

Black Creativity in Eroticism and Religion

Despite lethal blows in the construction of the black male body, African American men built creatively the foundation for their own self-identity. Theirs was a comprehensive creation of healthy eroticism and positive religiosity in the making of individual and collective body. In contrast, the larger system of American civil religion equated perversion and bestiality with black manhood. Black men, on the other hand, even with all their own shortcomings, laid the foundations of transcendent meaning within immanent manifestations. In a word, religion took on an ebony body. And this body displayed, acted out, and accepted eroticism. For our purposes of asserting the proactive posture of black male body construction, the definitions of eroticism and religion follow.

> EROTICISM: The powerful life force within us from which spring desire and creativity and our deepest knowledge of the universe. The life force that flows like an inscrutable tide through all things, linking man to woman, man to man, woman to woman, bird to flower, and flesh to spirit. Our ancestors taught us this in their songs of love, their myths of creation, their celebrations of birth, and their rituals of initiation. Desire. Pleasure. Wholeness.[35]

Eroticism speaks to black men's identity flooded with a life force in their very bodies. Here, eroticism distances itself from the dominating

---

34. Ibid., 28. Also examine Don Belton, "Introduction: Speak My Name," in *Speak My Name*, ed. John Belton, 1–5 (2).

35. Miriam DeCosta-Willis, "Introduction," in *Erotique Noire: Black Erotica*, ed. Miriam DeCosta-Willis et al. (New York: Anchor, 1992), xxix.

cultures and oppressive religion's planks in the building of the black male body. Yes, eroticism includes sex, yet it surpasses sex by situating it within a fluid and broader framework. Eroticism works itself from the inside out. The inside consists of a transcendent life force, an integrated spirituality clinging sensuously to flesh. The flow of the force of life is communal and interactive among human, animal, and plant life, as well as the natural elements. It recognizes its cornerstone as the holy history of black ancestors. Consequently, eroticism is history, knowledge, desire, pleasure, wholeness, and creativity.

And religion means orientation—"orientation in the ultimate sense, that is, how one comes to terms with the ultimate significance of one's place in the world. The Christian faith provided a language for the meaning of religion, but not all the religious meanings of the black communities were encompassed by the Christian forms of religion."[36] How does the black male body construct itself to come to terms with the ultimate (that is, the holy, the sacred) in its being, its consciousness, its feelings, and its doing? How does it start from the inside and overflow out into experience, rhythms, behaviors, styles, motivation, and intentions? That which is ultimate (in terms of life and death—meaning the sacred) lives in the body. It is life force. Religion, therefore, is erotic.

For example, Jesus Christ, in black Christianity, is body revelation of sacred life force. "Jesus Christ clearly signifies that God loves us not in spite of or apart from our bodies, but that God loves us in our bodies as uniquely embodied creatures."[37] Simultaneously, the blues moan and groan out another revelation of sacred life force. In the blues, physicality and spirituality connect as another expression of the life force among black citizens. African American people see a powerful "spiritual function of the human body." The sacred and the secular, the divine and human come together. "For black people the body is sacred, and they know how to use it in the expression of love."[38]

And so black men redesigned the definitions of eroticism and religion to create their own foundation in black male body construction. Specifically, a set of building blocks in the positive self creation of the black male body can be seen in an African American man's reworking of Alice Walker's

---

36. Charles H. Long, *Significations: Signs, Symbols, and Images in the Interpretation of Religion* (Philadelphia: Fortress, 1986), 7.

37. Kelly Brown Douglas, *Sexuality and the Black Church: A Womanist Perspective* (Maryknoll, NY: Orbis, 1999), 123.

38. James H. Cone, *The Spirituals and the Blues: An Interpretation* (New York: Seabury, 1972), 128.

idea of "womanism."[39] Learning from how black women have renamed themselves, African American men are creating a new type of masculinity.

1. From *High John the Conqueror*. A mode of masculinity for Black men who are committed to the liberation and survival whole of Black people. Inspired by a trickster figure in African American folklore also known as Jack who is the human analogue of Brer Rabbit. As a slave, John is a redemptive, transgressive, and resourceful figure who achieves advantages over 'Old Massa' through motherwit, laughter, and song. He lives in the slaves' quarters of plantations and in the conjure root that bears his name.

2. *Also*. A man of courage who routinely 'beats the unbeatable.' A man who laughs at himself and also understands the many uses of laughter. As the hope-bringer, a man who's been 'down so long that down don't bother' him. Unflappable. Responsible, as in: 'Takes care of business' or 'On the case.' Traditionally capable, as in: 'able to make a way out of no way and can hit a straight lick with a crooked stick.' A man of strength possessing confidence and a durable constitution as in: 'Ain't no hammer in dis lan strikes like mine.' Admirable and honorable as in: 'You de man.' (Opposite of trifling, jive, half-stepping, irresponsible, player, not serious).

3. In his youth: mannish. From the Black folk expression of elders to male children: 'You acting mannish.' i.e., like a man. Often referring to bodacious defiant, willful, and risky behavior, as in: 'He's smelling himself' or 'You trying to be grown.' Evincing a premature interest in adult activities and privileges.

4. Loves the Spirit. Loves men (sexually and/or nonsexually) and the society of men. Loves women (sexually and/or nonsexually) and the society of women. Loves children. Loves his ancestors. Loves difference. Loves creativity, song, and dance. Loves the beautiful/ugly. Loved by others: as in, 'My main man' or 'Show me some love.' Loves movement: as in, 'Gotta highball thru some country.' Loves himself. *Irregardless*.

5. Free, as in 'I ain't worried about that.' Spunky. Crazy but got good sense. Regular. Committed to coalitions, but capable of independent action. Nonviolent, but capable of self-defense.

---

39. Alice Walker, *In Search of Our Mothers' Gardens: Womanist Prose* (New York: Harcourt Brace Jovanovich, 1983), xi–xii.

Persevering and enduring as in 'Keep a-inchin' along lak a po' inch worm.' A man who flourishes in the 'Be class,' as: '*Be* here when the ruthless man comes and *be* here when he is gone.' Cool.

6. 'A bottom fish,' as in values knowledge, truth, and wisdom. Values process and improvisation. Values collective work and solitude. Values dialogue, listening, and harmony. Values tenderness. Values the strength in feelings and tears. Values freedom and its responsibilities. Values justice. Values peace.

7. A mode of masculinity for Black men who are committed to the abolition of emasculating forms of masculinity; a mode of masculinity for Black men who are committed to the abolition of racism, sexism, homophobia, and other ideological traps."[40]

I would say that this new mode of black masculinity is made up of at least healthy eroticism and empowering religion. We remember that eroticism is pleasurable life force internal to the body; this force draws on history, knowledge, desire, pleasure, wholeness, and creativity. And religion is orientation toward the ultimate in one's life and death. Thus, erotic religion or religious erotic of the black male body concerns the ultimate living in the body and a spirituality clinging to every dimension of flesh.

Part 1 of the above definition lifts up the black male identity as pro-liberation and survival whole of all black people. The black male body transcends itself, first of all, by being dedicated to the entire community. This allegiance equals a religious commitment or ultimate faith in the sense of one's life-and-death calling to be there for the entire extended family and not mainly focus on the individualism of the self. Commitment, faith, and ultimate suggest that part of being an African American male is to put one's black body on the line for others. The internal life force inspiring this liberation-survival commitment is made of definite aspects; that is, redemption, transgression, and resourcefulness. Moreover, a flesh life force of being present for other bodies helps the new mode of black masculinity to practice both survival (i.e., to make do within negative structures) and liberation (i.e., to transform radically entire systems and establish new ones).

To follow the life force within towards liberation and survival, furthermore, requires courage, part 2 of the definition. And a black male in America called to put his body on the line against nonintentional (i.e.,

---

40. Rudolph P. Byrd, "Prologue: The Tradition of John; A Mode of Black Masculinity," in *Traps*, 1–2.

liberal) and intentional (i.e., conservative) structures of white supremacy is either insane or courageous. By being there, in crisis and out of crisis, the visibly present black male body helps to spread hope, responsibility, strength, confidence, admiration, and honor.[41]

Part 3 honors the younger generation of black males. 'Mannish' is a word used between father figures and male youth. By seemingly criticizing overconfident youth, the elder male is actually teaching the young about what he is up against when the youth thinks, acts, and has faith like a man. In other words, the older figure is training the younger how to come to terms with the calling of the life force within his black male body, the spirituality clinging to the throbbing of his flesh. The boy needs to properly understand the implications of the sacred tradition of a man's erotic body, especially when "he's smelling himself."[42]

One of the most challenging aspects of the life force–flesh connection, for the grooming of young black males, is confusion about, volatility of, and ambiguity about love. For the flesh to experience the pleasures of a healthy eroticism, it must first accept the Spirit. This is the ultimate life force already present in the erotic black body. Love of the Spirit in oneself provides the condition for self body love and male-male, male-female body love (sexually and nonsexually). It increases love of the ancestors (i.e., the living dead), the unborn (i.e., those spirits preparing to enter the space of body flesh), and the children (i.e., the representatives of ancestral inheritance). The ultimate Spirit love, put differently, nurtures a universal love of all humans, plants, animals, and the natural elements. As a foundational plank, black men must love religiously their own erotic body "irregardless."[43]

A spirit filled body produces an outward love that sees and treats one's lover as a full independent human being. Referring to black men in hetero-erotic relations, we see deep and broad love in the following.

> The strength of a man isn't in the deep tone of his voice. It's in the gentle words he whispers. The strength of a man isn't in the

---

41. On the notions of staying, being there, and setting examples, see James Baldwin, *The Evidence of Things not Seen* (New York: Holt, 1995), 20–21; Arthur Flowers, "Rickydoc: The Black Man as Hero," in *Speak My Name*, 263; and Randall Kenan, "Mr. Brown and the Sweet Science," in ibid. 66.

42. Compare Dennis A. Williams, "A Mighty Good Man," in ibid., where he describes the reflections of a younger man on the older and young black male interchange: "I can only now begin to appreciate how much effort and genius that requires—to guide without commands, to correct without rebuke, to set limits without saying no" (84–85).

43. This type of love, I believe, would encourage more black men to stay in church and relish the company of their wives and, in the process, reaffirm their wives' authority. See Dennis A. Williams, "A Mighty Good Man," in *Speak My Name*, 24–25.

weight he can lift. It's in the burdens he can carry. The strength of a man isn't in how hard he hits. It's in how tender he touches. The strength of a man isn't in how many women he's loved. It's in how true he can be to one woman.[44]

Building a sacred erotic black male body with this perspective develops an understanding that love precedes sex. Sex, here, is the culmination of an ongoing sensuous body interchange of talking, reliability, and the unsolicited surprise. In a monogamous marriage, foreplay starts with the hug and kiss goodbye as one leaves the home in the morning. "Which was followed up by taking out the trash and dropping her clothes off at the cleaners. The foreplay was continued by the phone call in the middle of the day to see how her day was going, to removing the dinner plates from the kitchen table, and helping the children with their homework." A love of commitment to one's wife and allegiance to the Spirit will naturally lead to black bodies in spiritualized eroticism of the flesh.[45]

Parts 5 and 6 help us to recognize that freedom comes from the inside out. In this way, the black male body is never a slave. He might be *enslaved*, but still remain free within. Consequently, external chains of slavery do not determine the inner life force of the eroticized body. So he can "be here when the ruthless man comes and be here when he is gone." With this sense of what's in his body, a black man is free to leave options open from nonviolence to self-defense, from joint work to independent action. And the practice of the "bottom fish" offers the ethics of mutual values. That is to say, freedom on the inside allows for a both-and acceptance of seemingly polar opposites in the man's thought, talk, and walk.

Finally part 7 teaches us about ending the weak forms of insecure black masculinity. To build a black male body, one has to also repair foundational fault lines in black masculine identity. The struggle against the system of white supremacy cannot succeed if black men construct walls of hierarchy for the exclusion of others who experience similar barriers of oppression in their body lives. The fight against the power of racism and for healthy individual and collective masculine healing will succeed when the humanity of one individual depends on aiding the humanity of others. "Reading men in the context of race is thus a dialectical intervention: an attempt to understand men at the (construction) site of specific power relations, each

---

44. Sadie B. Gandy, "Blessed Boys!" in *What Keeps Me Standing: Letters from Black Grandmothers on Peace, Hope, and Inspiration*, ed. Denis Kimbro (New York: Doubleday, 2003), 181.

45. Elder Sharon T. Jones, "The Love We've Lost," in ibid., 205.

relation mediating the reproduction and transformation of another."[46] The new identity helps in the empowerment and health of working-class people, African American women, and black lesbians and gays. While all African American men experience the sinister, subtle, and shocking cases of white supremacist systems, black middle- and upper income, heterosexual male bodies live a status of privilege vis-à-vis the working class and the poor.[47]

And so the Spirit-grounded in flesh is a location of different power processes. A bottom-line question is whether the new mode of black masculinity leads to an equalization of resources and rights among African Americans as well as between the whole of black people and the dominating society. If we answer yes, we expand our own definitions of who we are and thereby destroy insecure masculinities. Therefore to struggle for the neighbor as well as the self opens the door to a new type of theology—that is, critical self-reflection on how Spirit dwells in flesh.

In other words, the construction of the black male body with a positive religion and healthy eroticism means seeing the implications of a theology of eroticism. "We must recover the erotic use of our bodies from the distortions of white racism and the traps of black exploitation. We must liberate ourselves to embrace the Christian bliss of our black bodies."[48] And we can quickly add that so-called secular black spirituality (seen in the creative genius of Marvin Gaye, Prince, Jimi Hendrix, and Lightnin' Hopkins) has already given into the seductive possibilities of the black male body in music and song. Actually the Saturday night black love of "oh, yes, baby, I'm yours, baby . . ." is not too far from the Sunday morning church irruptions of "oh, yes, Jesus, I'm yours, Jesus . . ." As long as the body focuses on the sacred life force within, both nighttime and daytime forms of erotic release point to a proactive, self-love and self-empowerment.

---

46. Michael Uebel, "Men in Color," in *Race and the Subject of Masculinities* ed. Harry Stecopoulos and Michael Uebel (Durham, NC: Duke University Press, 1997), 2.

47. Examine Marlon T. Riggs, "Black Macho Revisited: Reflections of a SNAP! Queen," in *Black Men on Race, Gender, and Sexuality*, 308; and Devon W. Carbado, "Introduction," in ibid., 4–9.

48. Michael Eric Dyson, "When You Divide My Body and Soul, Problems Multiply," in *Traps*, 313 and 316–17.

5

L.A. and the City: What's God Got to Do With It?

I would like to give my presentation at three levels: first, a reading of the use of violence on Rodney King's body; second, an examination of the reasons for the counterviolence after the verdict; and third, a theologically based framework for moving forward beyond violence and counterviolence.

Violence against the Black Body

On March 3, 1991 (in Los Angeles, California), three black men in a speeding car drove through red lights on freeway 210. In pursuit was a husband-and-wife team of the California Highway Patrol. When the speeding car eventually pulled over, twenty-one Los Angeles (L.A.) city police and two L.A. unified school district officers arrived. Rodney King, a twenty-five year old, six-foot African American male exited the car and in the testimony of some witnesses laughed, did a little dance, and grabbed his buttocks or crotch. In response, he received kicks, pushes, stun gun blasts, fifty-six blows, and a foot on his neck. Resultantly, King suffered "a split upper lip, a partially paralyzed face, nine skull fractures, a broken cheek bone, a shattered eye socket, and a broken leg." A lot of this beating was captured in eighty-one seconds on a video.[1]

The violence practiced on Rodney King's black body is nothing new in the democratic tradition and ethical heritage of the United States. The approach toward, display of, and disregard of the African American physical presence has its foundational and visceral beginning in the period of slavery, that time and space of legal white supremacy from 1619 to 1865. In

---

1. Quotes and statistics come from mainstream media during the time of the event.

other words, for two hundred fifty years, a specific attitude appeared in the very essence of the American self-definition that perceived and acted upon the black body as if it were expendable.

Discipline

During the era of American slavery, a white culture of disciplining the black body arose from legal and biblical interpretation and justification. For instance, by legal statute, South Carolina owners had to castrate any enslaved African American man who wanted freedom by running away. If the master did not perform this civic duty of white Americans, then the slave owner was subject to loss of the black property. Similarly, the northern state of New Jersey standardized its "gelding law" (i.e., castration) in 1706. On a parallel tract, Euro-American clergy stood in solidarity with politicians by ensuring the sacredness of violently removing a black man's reproductive organs. Some Baptists and Anglicans gave the following theological rationale:

> We apprehend, the Master Acting according to the Law of your Province, in gelding his slave, hath not committed any crime, to give any member to break communion with him in the church; because we see by Scripture, that 'tis lawful to buy them. Gen. 17:13, 23, 27. And if lawful to buy them 'tis lawful to keep them in order, and under government; and for self-preservation, punish them to prevent further mischief that may ensue by their running away and rebelling against their master. Exodus 21:20, 21.[2]

The Old Testament Genesis chapter, founded on God's making of all creation in goodness, and the Exodus chapter, noted for a primary theme of liberation of slaves from torture and forced labor, became verbal distortions for dismembering the black male sexual body. As early as the colonial days—the end of the 1600s and the beginnings of the 1700s—white sectors of economic and political powers followed a persistent pattern and institutionalized a suspicious attitude toward African American men's bodies by practicing intentional maiming. And white pastors, ordained by their interpretation of God's word, blessed this religious ceremony of violence theologically with a liturgy of biblical evidence. God gave power to destroy the black sexual organ as punishment for deeds done and as precaution against future crimes.

---

2. Margaret Washington Creel, *A Peculiar People: Slave Religion and Community-Culture among the Gullahs* (New York: New York University Press, 1988), 79–80.

Branding was a more common form of black bodily mutilation. Like the fate of cattle or sheep, African American workers were either tied or held down while the master had hot irons imprinted into their burning flesh. This control of the black body through forced desecration often took place at a very young age. Recalling the experience of this painful ordeal, a former slave stated: "When I was about 8 or 10 years old, my master burnt on my breast, with oil of vitriol, the letters of W.L." Other enslaved African Americans suffered branding identification techniques as forms of punishment for failing to fulfill the work expectations and quota for a day. In this instance, branding meant "cutting gashes into their skin."[3] Branding represented an exact ownership operation because the white master's name could be seen clearly on the flesh of the ebony body. A public display of permanent instruction for which master owned which slave, branding, moreover, served as an immediate badge distinguishing the racial, class, and caste dynamics in Protestantism and American culture. Perhaps the most damaging effect of this accepted procedure was the psychological boost in ego given to the white population—the maturing conscious and subconscious belief in the necessity of tearing apart the black body with impunity. Fundamentally, branding was a sign in the public arena, which offered the black body to be read as text for whites' truth about ownership and slaves' submission to that violent truth.

The environment of acceptability and habit of expecting the disciplining of the black body appeared further in the refined torture techniques perfected after numerous applications. One master dragged a live cat with claws extended over the prone body of an accused slave. "The cat sunk his nails into the flesh, and tore off pieces of the skin with his teeth." Then the master applied the cat, not from the prostrate accused shoulders down again, but from the waist up. In another instance, Lilburn and Isham Lewis, two nephews of Thomas Jefferson, slowly chopped up the body of a live slave as a lesson to prevent other chattel from running away. In a deliberate plan, one of the nephews hacked off the feet, paused to lecture the other slaves in attendance, continued by chopping off below the knees and then casting them into a fire and proceeding slowly with occasional lectures while the victim howled in pain, with finally nothing remaining except the head, which was likewise tossed in the flames.[4]

---

3. The eight-year-old's account is from *National Anti-Slavery Standard*, October 22, 1840, p. 78, found at Widener Library, Harvard University (Cambridge, Massachusetts) and the "gashes . . . skin" text comes from an interview with ex-slave Mrs. Florence Bailey, found in The John B. Cade Library Archives, Southern University (Baton Rouge, Louisiana), no page numbers.

4. The cat torture mechanism is found in *The Liberty Almanac*, no. Two, 1845,

However, to standardize the refined torture techniques, a comprehensive profit-making industry and imaginative repressive expertise arose exposing the role that disciplining the black body played in furthering technology and experimentation in American culture. One owner made a gradation of stocks, one on top another. When he accumulated enough guilty chattel, he placed them in the stocks above each other. "They would all be required to take a large dose of medicine and filth down upon each other." Old Mack Williams, another owner, developed chains, which he placed around black necks as fatal punishment; utilizing the chains, he would have the slaves thrown into a river and drowned. And in the words of a former slave: "My marster had a barrel with nails drove in it that he would put you in when he couldn't think of nothin' else mean to do." With the slave secure in the torture barrel, the owner would push it down a hill.

The most established industries of pain made various forms of "the runaway's irons." After fleeing and being captured, whipped for four days and left for four days in the stocks, a former slave named Lewis suffered the following:

> Early the next morning Lewis was taken out of his prison, and led by two men to the blacksmith's shop, to receive "the runaway's irons." An iron ring, weighing fourteen pounds, was welded on his ankle; and to that was fastened one end of a heavy log-chain, the other end of which was brought up and passed twice around his waist where it was secured by a lock. A collar was then put around his neck, from which an iron horn extended on each side nearly to the point of the shoulder.[5]

(Syracuse, New York, Tucker & Kinney, Publishers). And text of Thomas Jefferson's nephews can be read in *The American Anti-Slavery Almanac for 1840*, vol. 1, no. 5. Both documents are located at Cornell University, Slavery Collection.

5. See Peter Still and Vina Still, *Kidnapped and the Ransomed: The Narrative of Peter and Vina Still after Forty Years of Slavery* (1856; reprint, Philadelphia: Jewish Publication Society of America, 1970), 195. For the 'stock" reference, review former slave Robert Small's testimony in "Extracts from Debates on the Adoption of the Federal Constitution, Relating to Slavery" of the American Freedman's Commission, 1863–64, microfilm roll 200, no page number, at the Library of Congress. Regarding Old Mack Williams, refer to interview of ex-slave William Ward in George P. Rawick, ed. *The American Slave: A Composite Autobiography, Georgia*, v. 13, part 4 (Westport, CT: Greenwood, 1979), 133. The barrel citation comes from the same volume and part, p. 297.

Other references to the variations of the "runaway's irons" or "chokers" can be investigated in the "The Emancipated Slave face to face with his Old Master: Valley of the Lower Mississippi: Supplemental Report (B); American Freedmen's Inquiry Commissions by James McKaye p. 27, found at the National Archives in Washington DC, file 3280, 1863, roll 199.

Likewise, fugitive John Brown remembered the detailed features of the circles of iron, padlocks, rods, and bells strapped around his chin, forehead, and neck. "I wore the bells and horns, day and night, for three months," he wrote. "At night I could not lie down to rest, because the horns prevented my stretching myself, or even curling up."[6]

A group of businessmen—agreeing with the wishes of plantation owners, the policies of politicians, and the theological blessings of religious leaders—sat down to imagine the most efficient way to wrap iron around the necks, heads, waists, and limbs of black men and women in America. Measurements had to be taken. Bodies had to be fitted and refitted for precision. Pounds had to be calculated to ensure optimum weight and pain short of death. How to control the labor force through appropriately sized torture techniques must have necessitated trial-and-error experimentation. Consequently, a mindset unaffected by the breaking of black bones and skin created a worldview where pain for African Americans was believed to be in their best interests and for the nation's welfare. Blacksmiths and related businessmen reaped profits while African American chattel agonized in disfigurement; and the nation felt safe.

Perhaps the most daily brutality inflicted on the black body during slavery—the foundational period where Protestantism and American culture established its democratic etiquette of subduing the black body—was the whip. Here the intricate fascination with how to distort, contort, and cut up the African American physical body was regularized every day. There were at least four types of standard whips made specifically for blacks—the holed paddle (which could make blisters and then have the blisters filled with pepper), the ox whip (which was believed to handle any black male who had the strength of an ox), the bullwhip (an interchangeable delicacy which was applied both on African Americans and bulls), and the Negro whip. Fugitive William W. Brown, in his autobiography, describes the Negro whip: "The handle was about three feet long, with the butt-end filled with lead and the lash six or seven feet in length, made of cowhide, with platted wire on the end of it."[7]

---

6. This excerpt is from *Slave Life in Georgia: A Narrative of the Life, Sufferings, and Escape of John Brown, a Fugitive Slave, Now in England* (London, April 1865) edited by L. A. Chamerovzow, Secretary of the British and Foreign Anti-Slavery Society, London, is found in *The Anti-Slavery Advocate*, 257, at the Boston Public Library.

7. Brown in William Loren Katz, ed., *Five Slave Narratives* (New York: Arno, 1968). Reference to the holed paddle is found in an interview with former chattel Joe Johnson, in the Cade Library Archives, no page number; to the ox-whip in an interview with former slave Sam Gray in the John B. Cade Library Archives, Southern University (Baton Rouge, Louisiana), no page number; and to the bullwhip in Fisk University Social Science Institute, *Unwritten History of Slavery* (Nashville: Fisk University Social Science

Along with the four types of whips, a white citizen could then pick from a menu of five different whipping positions—the buck, the log, the stake, the tree, or the stocks.

In a word, the slavery system implanted in the American national psyche an equation between Christian duty and beating of the black body. Former slave Harriet Jacobs, in her autobiography, remembers this standard American democratic and theological tradition. "The [church] class leader was the town constable—a man who bought and sold slaves, who whipped his brethren and sisters of the church at the public whipping post, in jail or out of jail. He was ready to perform that Christian office any where for fifty cents."[8]

Thus the crushing blows and beating of Rodney King's body have a long background that has been absorbed in the United States' culture of beliefs and instincts. What is probably most extraordinary about that fateful event was that it was captured on eighty-one seconds of videotape.

Why Counterviolence?

From April 30th through May 2nd, 1992, in reaction to the violent beating of and Simi Valley court verdict against Rodney King, parts of urban America offered its own verdict of counterviolence by bringing on the fire of street justice. Though Seattle, Atlanta, Detroit, and other urban areas reacted, clearly it was the conflagration in Los Angeles that focused the world's attention and raised the question, why? Why was L.A. the worst civil unrest in U.S. history? Sixteen thousand two hundred ninety-one were arrested. Fifty-two were dead and 2,383 were injured. Over 1 billion dollars in property was damaged. Over five hundred fires burned. Law enforcement personnel numbering 22,720 were activated.[9] Why did L.A. explode? Clearly the immediate spark that ignited a literal city fire was the Simi Valley

---

Institute, 1945), 134.

As the Civil War unfolded, many observers in the South wrote letters to the federal government on the conditions of enslaved blacks. Regarding the types of whips used, one author wrote: "There was the whip of knotted hempen-cords; the whip with the twisted lash of dried bulls hide; the coach-trace whip and the paddle." Flat handsaws were also employed as whips. See page 18 of "The Emancipated Slave Face to Face with His Old Master: Valley of the Lower Mississippi: Supplemental Report (B); American Freedmen's Inquiry Commission by James McKaye," found in the Washington DC, National Archives, file 3289, 1863, microfilm roll 199.

8. Harriet Jacobs, *Incidents in the Life of a Slave Girl Written by Herself* (1861; reprint, Cambridge: Harvard University Press, 1987), 70.

9. These statistics come from mainstream publications during that time period.

verdict that cleared the policemen who attacked an unarmed Rodney King. But a more appropriate question would be, why did it take so long for L.A. and other urban areas to explode? To begin to respond to this question, we must use a multilevel interpretation.

On an economic level, it has to be recognized that an analysis of the African American reality comes out of the larger context of U.S. economic factors and concentration of wealth. For instance, in the U.S., 1 percent of the population owns 37 percent of the wealth. And 10 percent of the population owns 86 percent of the nation's wealth. Put differently, the historic and contemporary trends point to an ongoing redistribution of wealth from the bottom of society up to the top elite strata. Here, the crucial distinction is between wealth and income. Income is usually produced by one's individual ability to work for someone else or some other institution. In contrast, control of wealth means personal possession, either by an individual or a family, of capital and/or the interests and dividends generated by capital. If we were to use the commonsense metaphor of the shrinking pie of resources, we could say that 90 percent of U.S. citizens own only 14 percent of the country's wealth. And the very bottom 45 percent owns a mere 2 percent. Indeed the pie has shrunk for the overwhelming majority, while simultaneously the pie has increased and continues to increase for an extremely small few. Of all the industrial nations, the U.S. has by far the greatest inequality of wealth and resource distribution.

Furthermore, a class analysis of black America has to face a historic trend that has permanently changed the landscape—that is, the large, radical restructuring of the American economy. The early 1970s began to show the foundational crumbling of U.S. economic pillars, a disintegration which has continued until today. At the time of the 1970s, the U.S. dollar no longer enjoyed hegemony in the international market; this was a clear signal of domestic weakening as well. Basically, the productive boom of the 1960s began to slow down due to the shrinking income and resulting buying-power weakness of the non-wealth owning sectors of society. The inability to buy led directly to a percentage decline of rate of profit return.

The U.S. corporate sector also began to feel the growing and gnawing international competition. The strength of West Germany and Japan, in the areas of technology and automobiles, became very obvious in the U.S. domestic economy. Another crucial international indicator was the 1973 decision by industrial nations to give up the U.S. dollar as the standard international monetary rate of exchange. In addition in the mid-1970s, the OPEC (Organization of the Petroleum Exporting Countries) began to advance its united front in the field of oil by coordinating joint oil prices as leverage against the U.S. monopolization of monetary and capital resources.

During the 1980s, the U.S. economy hid this permanent and unique structural dislocation by borrowing heavily from other countries as well as from such domestic institutions as pension funds. Thus this new influx of real and paper money gave the appearance of an upswing in the domestic economy. Consequently, the 1980s was the decade of spending, building, and accumulation of massive debt primarily based on credit.

But now in the 1990s, the chickens are beginning to come home to roost. Today, the U.S. national debt, by the minute, is pushing beyond $4 trillion; that is to say, each American would have to pay $50,000 to get rid of this amount. Moreover, loans, debt, and credit obligations from the 1980s have started to become due. Corporations respond by attempting to restructure financial commitments, borrowing money to repay already borrowed money, and downsizing their businesses. Actually, the corporate sector prefers to call this latter move "rightsizing." Rightsizing means the permanent layoff of workers and taking back existing employee rights by, say, reducing health benefits and paid vacation time.

In addition, the new structural reality of shifting from the production of goods to the production of services and information technology has affected this chicken-coming-home-to-roost economic feature. Thus downsizing or rightsizing comes from the corporate drive to cut costs and, from their perspective, the need to re-equip themselves for the demands of an economy driven by service and information technology instead of one dominated by smokestacks from heavy industry.

From the start of this unprecedented structural realignment in the U.S. economy until today, for the first time in U.S. history, the upturn from regular economic crises did not produce a rehiring of previously laid-off workers. What this means is hoards of never-to-be-employed workers, symbolically speaking, begging outside the factory gates. This new dimension, among others, has led to a decrease in wages—a decrease of 15 percent in the last twenty years. An additional spinoff of the shift from the industrial to the service- and technology-driven market is the new demand for a workforce with more education and increased language, computer, and math skills. Large sections of the white American workforce suffered pain and hardship in this economic restructuring.

If white workers suffer such profound dislocations, one can imagine how the similar situation of African American workers will become even more permanent. Because the essential rearrangement in corporate economic policies mentioned previously has produced a disproportionate negative impact on black people, it is no accident that for the majority of African Americans their relative standard of living and quality of life are worse than they were before the 1950s and 1960s civil rights and black power movements. Disproportionately, blacks make up the first fired. Disproportionately, the black community has the biggest pain from this new reality of a permanent underclass. Disproportionately, the African American community has felt the extreme tensions, the absurdities of life, despair, and pressures from basic questions such as, where will so many black children get their next meals, let alone educational opportunities and a meaningful stable family life?

However, to talk of the black community today requires a more specific class analysis. This is important not only to understand the factual nature of the class and economic crisis, but also to see the multiple expressions of pain among too many black people.

We can describe black America as defined by several economic classes: a capitalist class, a middle-income class, a working and working-poor class, and a permanent unemployed class. The black capitalists make up roughly 14 percent (e.g., there are over four hundred thousand black-owned businesses. At the top extreme we find that three blacks are included in the list of the four hundred most wealthy Americans in the entire nation.) These capitalists appeal primarily to an African American market but also rely on a crossover appeal. Due to racial discrimination, they, moreover, suffer from lack of access to capital accumulation and expansion and, in everyday life, problems of housing denial, social immobility, and just plan disrespect.

The black middle-income group includes 17 percent—a class of professionals who do not survive mainly on capital ownership and who, at the same time, enjoy a salary base as opposed to wages earned. Sometimes they are one to two credit card payments away from significant financial dislocation if not repositioning into the working class, especially since quite a number of them used education to move from their family's working-class backgrounds. The vast majority of African Americans—44 percent—are working-class and working-poor wage earners. These are the people whose financial stability is slowly being eaten away due to the rapid rise in the cost of living; some in this class are on the border of living in the ranks of the permanently unemployed, particularly as the economy shifts to service and information technology production. They are the ones whose children are more and more being priced out of a college education. And they are the ones who are mostly victims of crime in the black community.

The last class is the unemployed. Here we find discarded workers, welfare recipients, and the underclass, who make up 25 percent of the total African American community. Restated, one-fourth of black Americans are permanently without legal jobs. Some are barely surviving on welfare payments, a below-minimum approach to human dignity. Some are living on soon-to-be-terminated unemployment benefits. Others are barely treading water with deflated retirement packages. And still others prey on the vulnerable through drug and various illegal industries.

Yet a class and race analysis of black America would be incomplete without brief attention to what we could call the hopelessness of "forced spiraling behavior" in the African American community. Poverty and racial discrimination have a fuller face than what has been quickly reviewed so far. It has a damning look that sees the black community spiraling further downward into despair and desperation. We could begin on the family level, where we discover that 56 percent of all African American households are headed by women, and 56 percent of these are below the poverty line. For the childbearing age group between fifteen and twenty-four, 68 percent of black children are born out of wedlock. Forty-one percent of African American teenage girls become pregnant by the age of eighteen. Nearly 40 percent of all black children live below the poverty line.[10]

Regarding black citizens being objects of the criminal justice system or its law enforcement mechanisms, African Americans make up over 40 percent of the inmates in state and federal prisons And 40 percent of death row inmates are black. Homicide is the number-one killer of young black men in the urban areas of America, further drowning black youth into the ever-present undercurrents of the criminal justice system and the morgue. Black males have a death rate 33 percent higher than black females. Those who do live suffer a one-in-three chance of not finishing high school; that is to say, over 33 percent of black youth drop out of school.[11]

But still the picture would not be complete without two additional diseases killing black potentiality—the twin demons of crack and AIDS. For black men, they are over three times as likely to die of AIDS than the national population. Black women experience a more tragic fate: They are over eight times as likely. In fact, the number-one killer of African American women twenty-five and under in the New York and New Jersey areas is AIDS. AIDS and crack are not simple physical evils, devastating the body into death. Moreover, they wear on families and neighborhoods, friendships and loyalties. They distort priorities where black babies are neglected and the positive meaning of life declines.

If these statistics of doom were applied to the U.S. on a national scale, the federal government, health officials, law enforcement agencies, corporate entities, and others would declare a national emergency. And herein lies a profound instance of systemic racial discrimination, which allows, by

---

10. These statistics come from mainstream publications during this article's time period.

11. These statistics come from mainstream publications during that time period.

purpose or design, American citizens to sink into a waste land and lack of dignity and humanity. Basically, an entire generation of black youth is withering away due to drug addition, deteriorating AIDS, homicide, unemployment, little formal education, neglect, and lack of love. Given such a sobering picture of deadly stories, how does the Rodney King affair help us to step back to vision new ways of moving forward?

Theologically Based Framework for the Future

Given the violence written on Rodney King's black male body and its foundation in U.S. slavery, and given the urban rebellion counterviolence and its larger implications, what theologically based framework can we suggest for the future?

Obviously Rodney King was a victim of representatives of a system and a culture that saw him as an animal. For instance, during the Simi Valley trial of the officers who attacked King, defense attorneys for the police portrayed King as the source of the danger, the police as endangered, and the beaten body on the ground in the eighty-one-second videotape as the source of the danger to twenty-three armed police personnel who stood around him. They stated that when King was stretched out on the ground with his hand up, he was actually suggesting potential danger—a suggestion representing not actual danger, but danger about to happen. The defense lawyers, furthermore, argued that Rodney King had "access to his hands, access to his legs." During the trial, the police officers referred to King as acting like a bear. A police paramedic described King as "belligerently spitting." Responding to a question, was King an animal, one officer said, "He just acted like one."[12]

While recognizing the victim status of King and of black America we have to at the same time raise a self-criticism. First, if we are to believe some of the witnesses, when he exited his car Rodney King's actions, symbolically, are negative realities in black America, which require African Americans to correct themselves and apply their own self-help remedies. It was stated that King was intoxicated, laughed, did a dance, and grabbed his buttocks or crotch. This type of drunken minstrelsy points to the negative ways how some in the black community respond to the larger racist structural attacks. God did not make black humanity in order for it to destroy itself through addiction to drugs or alcohol or both. God did not put black people on earth to participate in the destruction of the black family. It is one thing to

---

12. These statistics and quotations come from mainstream publications during that time period.

say that "the man" put drugs, AIDS, and guns in the black community, but, simultaneously, did God give black citizens the freedom to choose what to buy and use? Did God give African Americans the mental and intellectual ability to determine for themselves their own future?

From a wider angle of historical and current creativity, practices like faith, family, education, community, and self-help have been and remain fundamental to the survival, wisdom, and freedom options of millions of black grandparents, parents, and extended families from slavery until today.

Second, in addition to a full self-criticism and call for self-help (seen within how God has created black people as a positive people), one has to deal with African American female–male connections because both share equal original creation, and both have resources for liberation. Moreover, black women are at least half of the African American community and close to two-thirds of the black church. Both from the perspective of divine justice and mutual interdependent humanity, the faith experiences of black women and men must share in and act as sources for theological practices and material transformation. Perhaps when women are thoroughly included in the grassroots and national leadership levels, the potential of the New Jerusalem will begin to grow.

Third, the black community (in fact, all of the U.S.) needs to continue to develop a new language about what is "beautiful." Is beauty found in the criteria of exploitative market forces of monopoly capitalism or in the natural criteria given through God's grace? Specifically, there is a stepping back in the black community's definition of blackness as beauty or ugliness. In certain respects, in urban America, as one walks around the street, large segments of the black community are praising and worshiping a white Christian God as if the 1960s and 1970s black culture renaissance did not happen. Quite the contrary, not only does God sanctify black as beautiful (because black is the image of God), but African traditional societies have always accepted their own color and body. If black citizens are both God's people and African people in America, beauty is from God and ancestors.

Fourth, we need to deepen and practice a nonnegotiable value of prioritizing the collective, which comes from the African traditional worldview, the way of life of our grandparents and ancestors, and the Christian idea of connections through community. Certain African languages have very insightful and instructive greetings. When they meet one another, Africans can say one of two things or both. When they approach someone, they speak, "I see you," or "I see your family." The point is that they are expressing, recognizing, and affirming the fact that each person is defined by his or her relationship to their family. Thus individuality and community well-being both are complementary. Note that individualism, as opposed to individuality, is avoided.

Fifth, a sense of vocation needs to permeate the black community at all class levels. There should be a communal mission of a calling, responsibility, or vocation that defines the individual self; that is, a human being, and not an animal, operates in service to others. God has not created African American humanity to take on the life of the rugged individualist whose self-perception removes him from society in some fantasy response to the call of the wild. Nor has the divine created black people to follow a solitary life of a meditating hermit off alone seeking to arrive at full but lonely humanity of the individual self.

Sixth, the L.A. counter-violence further clarified the importance of coalition building. Of the people arrested, 36.9 percent were Latinos, 29.9 percent black, 6.8 percent white, and 26.4 percent of unknown racial or ethnic background.[13] Of course there remain some issues needing clarification, criticism, and correction within the black community. At the same time, one has to realize how God's people (i.e., the marginalized rainbow colors in America) come in all shapes and sizes. In fact, the ability to create a constructive reality with diverse neighbors indicates the maturation of self-confidence and self-love among black people. And coalition building stands not simply as a domestic agenda but as a part of the Pan-African and global strategic planning. The future of the black community and its children appears in an intricate, unbreakable project on the world stage. Thus coalition alliances link homeland and foreign territories.

Finally, biblical stories and African traditional society's practice of political economy show a way forward. Examining both Africa before the European contact and influence, as well as the book of Acts, we discover how societies provided for the well-being of all members. To be human means first concern for the health of all members of one's family and community. Such a faith and practice reveal how when one hungers or feasts, all huger or feast. When one rejoices in riches or suffers in poverty, all suffer the same condition together. Human beings, not God, created each society on earth, and human beings can transform those social relationships based on a common vision. No technology, no innovation, and no political policies remain forever.

---

13. These statistics come from mainstream publications during that time period.

Conclusion

In fact, to sum up what does God have to do with the challenges and opportunities revealed in Los Angeles, we conclude the following: Theologically the last and final goal for the new Cities of Angels and the New Jerusalem depends on the relationshiop between communalism and full humanity. It is a spiritual vision of a full humanity to which God has called all humanity—a vision of both a new heaven and a new earth, a plan for free spaces and peaceful times. Economically the realized final endpoint practices communal sharing because all creation is a gift from the divine to all human beings. In the beginning it was that way, but the sin of the human political economy of hoarding allowed a small group of families to monopolize the wealth at the expense of the overwhelming majority of the global population. Now human beings can change that political economy to reveal divine Spirit on behalf of all families.

Politically, the new vision means democracy, a new democracy in contrast to the old style. Restated, decision-making begins with the voices and priorities of the majority of the earth; that is to say, the working and poor humanity. Similarly, the ideal has the majority of elected representatives coming from these classes in society. A key element in the real majority social arrangements will be the easy ability to recall officials whose interests become antidemocratic. At its root, political democracy unleashes the constructive wisdom given by God to poor and working-class people.

Equality, the third strand within the full-humanity vision, means being self-critical and self-judging, grounded on what neighbors (i.e., those different from ourselves) have or do not possess. The crucial equality condition helps the collective to define and create a society where all have opportunities to share in abundant natural resources and accumulated technologies. Equality ties economics and politics; one has equal voice in society and equal access to earth, air, and water. Put another way, equality brings about the realization of our neighbors' gifts that God has granted them.

The new future human being and social relations operate on an empowering spirituality, which builds community interactions and creative individuality, not individualism. Specifically, all values creating a way of life and lifestyle of "I am because we are" will cover the new earth. Rather than "I think therefore I am," or "I have the right to make absolute money therefore I am," we presuppose God's creative intent is to have balance and harmony in society. A rhythm of being in the world means a proper interplay between each person, achieving full capabilities while at the same time the entire society benefits. Whenever neighbors or the neighbor suffers from the missteps or wicked words of someone else, then balance and harmony have been damaged and broken. The sins of human disorder would, at that point, challenge God's favorable order.

Finally those in the new social rearrangement will respect and reaffirm the particularity of each people's artistic identity. Specifically, a vision of a full humanity will accent the best in the African self; for the divine created blackness as an elegance of beauty.

Essentially, what we want are the technological, cultural, economic, spiritual, political, linguistic, social, artistic, and poetic conditions to help each person reach full potential. Short of that, not only will we betray the trust living in us on behalf of our children and our unborn, but the fire next time from future turbulent Los Angeles, to paraphrase James Baldwin, might consume all our white, black, yellow, red, and brown bodies. We are all in this together, so let's live together.

Part 2:
The Black Man and Black Women

6

Black Theology of Liberation and the Impact of Womanist Theology

Stages of Black Liberation Theology

Black liberation theology started on July 31, 1966, when a group of black pastors (who, at that time, self-described as Negro) connected the positive message of Jesus, African American culture, and justice for poor and working-class communities.[1] Their institutional creation of the ad hoc National Committee of Negro Churchmen in 1966 began stage 1 of black theology in which African American clergy attempted to separate the theological reflection and practice of black religion from that of the conservative and liberal theologies of the white churches. Thus, black theology started as a criticism both of white conservative theology's rejection of the role of the black church in the civil rights movement and of white liberal theology's denial of the relation between black religion and black power. Black theology put forth liberation of the oppressed as the key thread throughout the Christian gospel. For the creators of contemporary black theology, the good news of Jesus Christ was not neutral; Christianity concerned power—those with it and those without.

---

1. For different interpretations of the development of black liberation theology, see Gayraud S. Wilmore, general introduction to *Black Theology: A Documentary History, 1966–1979*, ed. Gayraud S. Wilmore and James H. Cone (Maryknoll, NY: Orbis, 1979); Wilmore, general introduction to *Black Theology: A Documentary History, 1966–1979*, ed. Gayraud S. Wilmore and James H. Cone (Maryknoll, NY: Orbis, 1993); James H. Cone, *For My People: Black Theology and the Black Church* (Maryknoll, NY: Orbis, 1984), chapter 1; and Dwight N. Hopkins, introduction to *Cut Loose Your Stammering Tongue: Black Theology in the Slave Narratives*, ed. Dwight N. Hopkins and George C. L. Cummings (Maryknoll, NY: Orbis, 1991).

Stage 2 of black theology began in 1970, with the creation of the Society for the Study of Black Religion. Black theology developed itself as an academic discipline in graduate schools, where black religious scholars emphasized religious issues among themselves. By this time, a trickle of African American professors had been allowed into divinity schools and seminaries. They struggled over themes such as the relation between liberation and reconciliation, God's goodness and human suffering, African religion and black theology, and the spontaneous faith expressions of African American people versus the theological systems of white graduate schools.[2]

More discussion took place about the non-Christian examples and movements that also represented black theology. In brief, God's liberation for the least in society showed itself through Jesus the Christ (for Christians). But this same spirit also appeared wherever liberation took place for oppressed people suffering internal, spiritual pain and external, structural exploitation. Although black theology turned more toward an academic emphasis in this phase, various historic black church hierarchies also began to respond favorably to different doctrines of the theology.

Stage 3, in the mid-1970s, gave birth to a new organization called the Black Theology Project (1975)—made up of church persons, community activists, and scholars—with a strong connection between African Americans and the Third World. The broad range of participants in this new group reflected black theology's turn toward liberation theologies in the Third World and a brief look at forms of African socialism, the day-to-day survival issues in the black community, black theology's relation to the African American church, and the importance of feminism and Marxism.

The fourth stage started around 1979–1980 when the first generation began to produce doctoral students. This period includes new voices concerned with both Christian and non-Christian aspects of black life, especially in African indigenous religions, modified African religious practices (in the Caribbean and Latin America), and black Islam. Furthermore, the increase of more pastors and professors studying and preaching black theology defines this fourth stage. And most strikingly is the cutting-edge challenge of womanists. These black female religious scholars pushed for a complete black theology that integrated race, class, gender, sexual orientation, and ecological analyses. Womanists also have shown the necessity of doing black theology from such new sources as African American fiction and women's roles in the Bible.

---

2. See Wilmore, general introduction, *Black Theology* (1979), 5.

Womanist Theology

One of the most important and innovative creations in the method of black theology is the rise of womanist theology. Womanist theology started within black theology, but now it invents its own faith practice and intellectual discipline. The roots of this theological process go back to the late 1970s and early 1980s, when black female graduate students at Union Theological Seminary in New York began to raise questions about the silencing or oppression of women in African American churches and in black theology.

Womanist theology is the phrase chosen by black female religious scholars, pastors, and laywomen who wish to name and claim two things: (1) the positive experiences of African American women as a basis for doing theology and ethics and (2) the separation of black women from both the racism of white feminist theologians and the sexism of black male theologians. Womanist theology grows out of black theology and therefore has separate theological beliefs from white feminist theology, which ignores racism. In this way, womanist theologians join with their black brothers in the struggle against the structures of white supremacy in the church, the society, and the schools. The experience of being black in America unites womanist and black theologies.

At the same time, their female gender experience in patriarchal America lays a basis for black women's coalition with white feminists. African American female religious scholars have to live out their dual status of race and gender before God. Womanist theology affirms the unique connection between God and black women and must struggle against white supremacy and black patriarchy.

Womanist theology, moreover, takes its theological guidelines from the definition of *womanist* given by Alice Walker in her 1983 book, *In Search of Our Mothers' Gardens: Womanist Prose*.[3]

Womanist

1. From womanish. (Opp. of "girlish," i.e., frivolous, irresponsible, not serious.) A black feminist or feminist of color. From the black folk expression of mothers to female children, "You acting womanish," i.e., like a woman. Usually referring to outrageous, audacious, courageous or willful behavior. Wanting to know more and in greater depth than is considered "good" for one. Interested in grown-up doings. Acting grown up. Being grown up. Interchangeable with

---

3. New York: Harcourt Brace Jovanovich, 1983, xi–xii.

another black folk expression: "You trying to be grown." Responsible. In charge. Serious.

2. Also: A woman who loves other women, sexually and/or non-sexually. Appreciates and prefers women's culture, women's emotional flexibility (values tears as natural counterbalance of laughter), and women's strength. Sometimes loves individual men, sexually and/or nonsexually. Committed to the survival and wholeness of entire people, male and female. Not a separatist, except periodically, for health. Traditionally universalist, as in: "Mama, why are we brown, pink, and yellow, and our cousins are white, beige, and black?" Ans.: "Well, you know the colored race is just like a flower garden, with every color flower represented." Traditionally capable, as in: "Mama, I'm walking to Canada and I'm taking you and a bunch of other slaves with me." Reply: "It wouldn't be the first time."

3. Loves music. Loves the moon. Loves the Spirit. Loves love and food and roundness. Loves struggle. Loves the Folk. Loves herself. Regardless.

4. Womanist is to feminist as purple to lavender.

Walker's four-part definition contains aspects of tradition, community, self, and a commonality with as well as a criticism of white feminism.

Womanist History

Womanist theology has a history that grows out of both the 1970s white feminist irruptions and the 1950s and 1960s black civil rights and black power awakenings. As the civil rights struggle picked up momentum and limited victories, white feminists began to push more strongly for the passage of the Equal Rights Amendment in the late 1960s and 1970s. The results of the feminist movement, from the perspective of womanists, meant at least two things: the increased presence of white women in various jobs and in seminaries and the realization by black women that racism still persisted in feminist coalitions. Although black women were obviously female, they still experienced racial hierarchy in their jobs and professions with white women.

Similarly, in the 1950s civil rights and 1960s black power movements, African American women faced patriarchy from African American men. The classic story describes a meeting between Stokely Carmichael, then chair of the Student Nonviolent Coordinating Committee (SNCC), and some of its black women members during the late 1960s. In this conversation the black women raised questions about the fair treatment and recognition of women in the organization; Carmichael's response was that the only position for black women in the movement was a "prone" position. It is precisely this type of oppressive attitude and exploitative practice that quite a number of black men carried into seminaries. Just as white women were increasing their numbers in graduate schools of religion, so were black men. When African American women slowly began to enter theological schools, a sizable number of African American men resisted women's desires to receive ordination and denied black women's calling by God.

Amid such an adversarial culture, the first article published from a womanist theological perspective was actually pointing toward black feminist theology. The young author, Jacqueline Grant, was a PhD student in systematic theology at Union Theological Seminary in New York. In 1979 Grant published her article titled "Black Theology and the Black Woman." Though the specific phrase *womanist theology* was created several years after this 1979 essay, historically this is the first essay that began womanist theology.

Grant's essay called into question the most fundamental belief of black theology as a theology of liberation. It challenged African American men's apparent overconfidence in liberation by illustrating how black theology contradicted its own criteria. Specifically, Grant argued that if black theology described itself as a theology of liberation—meaning that Jesus Christ was with the most oppressed, and God was working for the liberation of the least in society—then why was it that black theology, at best, was silent about African American women and, at worst, oppressed black women? The point was clear: Black theology cannot claim to be for justice and simultaneously treat black women as second-class citizens. In this article, Grant also drew lines of theological demarcation with white feminist theologians, but she emphasized that her primary focus was the development of an African American woman's voice in black theology.

Grant concluded that black women are invisible in black theology. She observed two derogatory justifications dominating the classroom: (1) African American women have no place in the study of God-talk and God-walk, and (2) black men are capable of speaking for black women. Similar conclusions can be drawn about black women in the African American church and the larger society. Grant wrote the following criticism of black religious institutions: "If the liberation of women is not proclaimed, the church's proclamation cannot be about divine liberation. If the church does not share in the liberation struggle of black women, its liberation struggle is not authentic. If women are oppressed, the church cannot be 'a visible manifestation that the gospel is a reality.'"[4]

The very first written work to use the term *womanist* was Katie G. Cannon's 1985 article "The Emergence of Black Feminist Consciousness." Championing Alice Walker's concept of "black womanist consciousness," Cannon observed that black feminist consciousness may, in fact, be more accurately defined as black *womanist* consciousness. Cannon writes how the black womanist tradition

> provides the incentive to chip away at oppressive structures, bit by bit. It identifies those texts that help Black womanists to celebrate and to rename the innumerable incidents of unpredictability in empowering ways. The Black womanist identifies with those biblical characters who hold on to life in the face of formidable oppression. Often compelled to act or to refrain from acting in accordance with the powers and principalities of the external world, Black womanists search the Scriptures to learn how to dispel the threat of death in order to seize the present life.[5]

Cannon's scholarship introduced womanism as the pioneering and new description for all black women's religious work; however, the first written text using the specific phrase *womanist theology* was by Delores S. Williams. In "Womanist Theology: Black Women's Voices," which appeared in the March 2, 1987, edition of *Christianity & Crisis,* Williams used Alice Walker's definition of womanism as a theoretical framework for black women's theology.[6]

Method in Black Liberation Theology

Womanist theology eventually created a specific method. Still, since it came out of black liberation theology, we start with the latter and then examine the creative outline of womanist methodology. Method in theology responds to the questions: How do people arrive at answers in their talk about and practice with God among the poor? How do they come to conclusions

---

4. In Wilmore and Cone, eds., *Black Theology: A Documentary History, 1966–1979,* 423.

5. Katie G. Cannon, "The Emergence of Black Feminist Consciousness," in *Feminist Interpretation of the Bible,* ed. Letty M. Russell (Philadelphia: Westminster, 1985), 40.

6. Williams's article "Womanist Theology: Black Women's Voices," can be found in *Black Theology: A Documentary History, 1980–1992,* ed. Wilmore and Cone.

about relations among God, humanity, and world? What sources are their starting points, what are their standard presuppositions, and what are the consequences of their theology? As a liberation theology, black theology is a systematic and constructive movement arising from the reality of God's emancipating power that thrives in all parts of life. God is present in all sources or aspects of black existence, especially that of the poor.

The Bible presents an abundance of stories about human tribulations and triumphs, and such sacred tales enrich immensely black theology's creativity. Today's poor African Americans have a parallel message of oppressed conditions and struggle for freedom to that of stories in the Hebrew and Christian Scriptures where Yahweh compassionately hears and sees the extreme difficulties faced and experienced by the bottom of society, in this case, the ancient Israelite slaves. When people living in a system of poverty today, read the story of enslaved ancient Israelite workers and their relationship to a liberator God, they can see that they are not alone in their cruel predicament in contemporary America.

The exodus story offers a picture of a similar people who suffered at the hands of brutal taskmasters; were accused falsely; were pursued by forces of prejudice; suffered through a wilderness experience; went through periods of anxiety, fear, and doubt about the future; at times longed for a return to their former status in an inhuman system; argued with their leaders; and yet doggedly pursued the way to freedom.

Moreover, the African American poor, reading the Hebrew Scriptures from their location on the underside of American society, discover a whole new world different from the dominating Christianity and theology of mainstream American believers. The exodus story does not end with harsh difficulties. On the contrary, the hope of deliverance cancels out the pain and energizes today's poor to keep on keeping on. The certainty of victory, found in the Hebrew Scriptures, empowers the poor in the midst of their deepest self-doubt.

Likewise, the black poor bring their own life issues to the stories in the Christian Scriptures. And Jesus meets and greets them as their liberator, the one who can perform miracles—turning the impossible into the possible. The lowly birth of Jesus; his singular purpose to be with, struggle with, and set free the oppressed; his constant harassment by the official authorities who questioned his goal to bring in a new society for the least in his day; his eventual death approved by government leaders and the police; and his final triumph of resurrection all bring hope, a sense of possibilities, and power for the poor. And so the first source of black theology is the relationship between the positive promise of justice and freedom found in the Bible, on one hand, and a similar thirsting for a new way of believing and living experienced by African American poor people today.

For black theology, the black church brings together the believers in the biblical stories of spiritual and material freedom. The African American church is still the most organized institution controlled solely by black people. The black church is black power. It is made up predominantly of poor and working people, of which up to 70 percent are women. Its class and gender composition provides a fertile basis for the development, construction, and implementation of a black theology of liberation, because African American women are usually at the bottom of American society, and the black church is often located in the heart of the black community. Its vibrant and holy worship experience helps its members to renew their spiritual and emotional strength into forms of self-respect and "somebodyness," vital ingredients for survival and protracted self-development.

Its language and rhythm of preaching, praying, and testifying empower the cultural aspects of black life, thus validating that black English, call-and-response rituals (or talking back to the preacher), and black folk's ways of thinking are worthy and authentic. Its economic resources and other forms of wealth (buildings, publishing centers, transportation vehicles, auditoriums, dining facilities, credit unions) on a national scale could offer an independent financial base for an alternative way of living in a society that continually makes black life and labor expendable.

Following the church and the Bible, a faith tradition of struggle for liberation makes up the third area from which to develop a black theology. Of course, the black church contains within its heritage a strong history of justice preaching and practice, starting from the indigenous religions of the first Africans forced to the "New World," through the invisible institution of slave religion, until today when liberating Christianity can be found in some local African American churches. At the same time, a faith tradition of struggle has existed outside formal church structures, most notably in the various periods of justice work of black civic, cultural, student, women's, and political organizations. God has offered the grace of freedom wherever God has chosen to freely give freedom. The possibilities of a liberated life extend beyond institutional religion.

African American women's experience constitutes the fourth source. If black women are the overwhelming majority of black church members and over half of the African American community, then black theology must speak to and reflect the intellectual and emotional concerns and contributions of women. A black theology without African American women would not be a complete and real theology. Indeed, black theology would be hypocritical if it claimed that God was for the liberation of all people yet supported only the minority, male members within the community and church.

Finally, black theology draws on the endless well of black culture—art, literature, music, folktales, black English, and rhythm. Liberation themes in non-explicit Christian stories have always been with African Americans. For example, one thing, among many, that crossed the Atlantic Ocean from the west coast of Africa to American slave colonies was the heroic and unending efforts of Anansi the spider, passed on through storytelling. Anansi the spider represents the small and powerless being able to outsmart those with power and survive. Jazz, too, periodically served as a creative and unique form of protest, refusing to fit within the stiff styles and linear themes of European and Euro-American music. Black people's unique approach to sports, including a celebratory and in-your-face flair, has presented a declaration of "I am somebody" in a world controlled by others of a different class and color. The extended family, arguably another art form, provided a way of life of survival and maintenance but also became a place to groom and affirm the minds of the young who could possibly one day become another Maggie Lena Walker,[7] John W. Rodgers Jr., Harriet Tubman, Sojourner Truth, Martin King, or Malcolm X. Liberation culture is vital for a constructive black theology.

Yet what is it that interweaves throughout any source of black theology that makes this form of God-talk and God-walk liberation? It is the presence of the Spirit of liberation itself that gives life to and judges the usefulness of each source. The theologian holds up this spirit as the yardstick to measure all the sources and asks, where can examples of liberation be found in these sources?

Method not only includes various sources and the yardstick of liberation but also the rhythm of doing black theology, which starts from a prior commitment to and practice with the poor in the African American community. From a social location within the black poor, theology then moves to working in solidarity with all racialized and ethnic poor people. How faith is practiced defines the first part of the rhythm. Because the spirit of comfort, hope, and liberation already exists among the marginalized in society even before the theologian works with them, the theologian has to get involved with this life-giving movement between the poor and a liberating spirit.

From a relationship with the poor and their concerns, theology develops as a second step within the rhythm of black theology. Theology, in

---

7. Gertrude Woodruff Marlowe, *A Right Worthy Grand Mission: Maggie Lena Walker and the Quest for Black Economic Empowerment* (Washington, DC: Howard University Press, 2003).

fact, is systematic, self-critical, and constructive thinking about the practice and faith of liberation of grassroots people within and outside the church. Theology involves that phase where the theologian, in community, pauses to think intentionally and self-consciously about whether or not the theologian and community are being faithful to what the Spirit of liberation has called them to do, think, believe, and feel.

The third dimension of black theology's methodological rhythm is the return of theology to the practice of faith to further the pastoral, ethical, political, cultural, economic, linguistic, and everyday way of life of the black poor trying "to make a way out of no way" with their liberator God. And the rhythm continues. We start with the practice of faith, move toward thinking about theology, and return to the practice of faith. The key at each moment depends on whether the Spirit of freedom is present or not for all of humanity, nature, and the cosmos.

Method in Womanist Theology

The arrival and advancement of womanist theological method gifts an important contribution to black liberation theology, the church, and the larger society. In the development of theology and ethics, womanists talk about an inclusive or total relation to the divine. For them, this means that African American women cannot be focused on one issue. So they speak about positive sacred-human connections around issues such as gender, race, class, sexual orientation, and, to a certain degree, ecology. In fact, an inclusive method and an inclusive worldview define what it means to do womanist theology, which accepts and uses the many theological examples of oppression and liberation, many disciplines and analyses, and the diverse dimensions of what makes up a human being—that is, the spiritual, cultural, political, economic, linguistic, and other parts.

Furthermore, in the words of Delores S. Williams, womanist theological method is "informed by at least four elements: (1) a multidialogical intent, (2) a liturgical intent, (3) a didactic intent, and (4) a commitment both to reason and to the validity of female imagery and metaphorical language in the construction of theological statements."[8]

Multidialogical intent allows Christian womanists to participate in many conversations with partners from various religious, political, and social communities. In these discussions, womanists focus on the "slow genocide" of poor African American women, children, and men caused by systems of exploitation. *Liturgical intent* helps black female religious scholars to create

8. Williams, "Womanist Theology," 269.

a theology relevant to the black church, especially its worship, action, and thought. At the same time, womanist theology confronts the black church with prophetic and challenging messages coming out of womanist practices. Black church liturgy has to be defined by justice. *Didactic intent* points to the teaching moment in theology as it relates to a moral life grounded in justice, survival, and quality of life considerations. All of these concerns can yield a language that is both rich in imagination and reason and also filled with female story, metaphor, and imagery.

The method of womanist theology includes both epistemology and practice—that is, how we obtain knowledge and how we practice our ethics. How do womanists get their knowledge, and how does knowledge relate to their practice? In the analysis of Kelly Brown Douglas, womanist theology is accountable to ordinary women—poor and working-class black women. Accordingly womanists must reach beyond the seminaries and divinity schools and go into churches and community-based organizations in order for womanist theologians to make theology more accessible. And if womanist theology is accountable to church and community-based women, then womanist conversations must take place beyond the schools; womanist theology must have as its primary talking partners and primary location poor and working-class women and their realities in churches and community organizations. Moreover, womanist theology must work with church women to help empower them generally and to assist them in creating change in the church leadership. African American women make up to 70 percent of black churches and are the financial supporters and workers of the church.[9]

Summing up the complete or inclusive foundations of the various sources in womanist theology, Emilie M. Townes states that the cornerstone of womanist belief and practice is the black church and larger community. From this environment, womanists learn from sacred and secular black writers and singers, conversations in higher education, black folktales, and even vodun and West African indigenous religions.[10]

For instance, one of the most creative models for practicing womanist theological method was initiated by Teresa L. Fry.[11] From 1988 to 1994, in

9. Kelly Brown Douglas, *The Black Christ*, The Bishop Henry McNeal Turner Studies in North American Black Religion 9 (Maryknoll, NY: Orbis, 1994), 114.

10. Emilie M. Townes, "Introduction," in *A Troubling in My Soul: Womanist Perspectives on Evil and Suffering*, ed. Emilie M. Townes, The Bishop Henry McNeal Turner Studies in North American Black Religion 8 (Maryknoll, NY: Orbis, 1993), 2.

11. Teresa L. Fry, "Avoiding Asphyxiation: A Womanist Perspective on Intrapersonal and Interpersonal Transformation," in *Embracing the Spirit: Womanist Perspectives on Hope, Salvation, and Transformation*, ed. Emilie M. Townes, The Bishop Henry McNeal Turner Studies in North American Black Religion 13 (Maryknoll, NY: Orbis, 1997), chapter 6. All references to Fry's work are from this article.

Denver, Colorado, Fry worked with African American women in churches, individual interest groups, and various other organizations. In this model, participants ranged from five hundred to six hundred. Fry states that the women created S.W.E.E.T. (Sisters Working Encouraging Empowering Together), which was an intentional womanist effort to support black women's spiritual and social liberation. The project was truly inclusive: ages six or seven through seventy-eight; educational levels from grade school to graduate school; women who were married, widowed, single, and divorced; heterosexual, lesbian, and bisexual members participated; faith perspectives from ecumenical to interfaith to unchurched to personalized spiritual feelings appeared; some who "had been incarcerated, on the way to jail or knew someone there" became part of it; and "Deltas, Alphas, Zetas, Sigmas, and Links sitting alongside Granny, MaDear, Mama, Big Momma, and Auntie."

S.W.E.E.T. organized

> annual seminars, inclusive seminars, intensive women centered Bible studies, monthly workshops, relationship building exercises, small group discussions, potluck dinners, informal and formal luncheons, community action projects, intergenerational mentoring groups, individual and group counseling sessions, guest speakers, and in group speakers, panel discussions, role playing, ethnographies, health support groups, and African American women's literature study and discussion groups. Alice Walker's definition of womanist was used as the point of departure of each discussion.[12]

The following was added to Walker's definition: a S.W.E.E.T. womanist also "believes in Somebody bigger than you and me" or "possesses a radical faith in a higher power."

Throughout the sessions, women were encouraged to think for themselves and form their own opinions and models of life by taking seriously their own experiences. In addition, each person had a chance to lead meetings. One rule governed all of S.W.E.E.T.'s activities: "We will respect our sister's space, speech, issues, voice, pain and sensitivities." Women used titles such as Sister and Girlfriend, or first names. And elders were respected with the designation of Mother (for the spiritual anchors of the group) or Miss.

> Women were not pressured to be a member of a church and there was an understanding that the group was spiritually based. Each sister determined and articulated her own sense of spirituality. African American spirituality is the conscious awareness of God, self, and others in the total response to Black life and

---

12. Ibid., 80.

culture. It is the expressive style, mode of contemplating God, prayer life, and that which nourishes, strengthens and sustains the whole person. We coupled prayer, testimony, tears, laughter, or silence with embracing each other.[13]

Further S.W.E.E.T. activities included interviews with members' mothers and grandmothers, and with other mothers; investigations of black women leaders in different fields and in history; discussions on how to change and save the black family based on African family values; interviews with black clergywomen in the pulpit, revisioning inclusive liturgies, and seeing women's roles in the Bible; "Back to the Kitchen Table" programs held on Saturday mornings in different homes; an intergenerational group, "It Takes an Entire Village to Raise a Child"; and "Loving and Care for Yourself" gatherings about preparing for and recovering from a hysterectomy, about living with breast cancer, about experiencing divorce, about living as or with new Christians, about parenting as single mothers, about exercising, and about practicing self-affirmation.

So far we have looked at the origin of black theology, its stages of development, its themes, its method, and the challenge and contributions of womanist theology. However, another question needs an answer: What is the role of the church and its relation to black theology and womanist theology?

The Hope of the Future

The main institutional hope for African American people remains the black church, which is still the oldest, most organized, most spirit-supporting community for black life and for potential radical social transformation. The church is called to act on several different levels. On a pastoral level, the church is called to minister to the pain and brokenness of a people who are being wounded and are wounding themselves. It is called to witness as a religious institution to practice concrete ways to help the poor "to make a way out of no way." On a theological level, the church is called to witness, in its way of life, the presence of hope of a righteous God who reveals Godself through the love, hope, and liberation of Jesus the Christ. On a prophetic level, the church is called to speak truth to the powerful in America so that those who are put down by the mighty of society will know that there is a balm in Gilead that binds the brokenhearted and battered bodies of the poor.

13. Ibid., 81.

Therefore, the most promising pockets of hope on the local level are those few black churches and church-related institutions that preach and practice an inclusive and complete approach to theology and Christian practice. Specifically, they get involved in all parts of black people's lives, from political organizing to baptizing new believers. These churches have developed a prophetic ministry while impacting both the margins and the mainstreams. In a sense, they are the African American mirror of South America's basic Christian communities made up of peasants and workers concerned with social change and personal salvation.

The pockets of hope found in prophetic black churches serve as pointers to possibilities of social and individual transformation for African Americans affected by class, race, and gender in the United States. Each local example shows us seeds of what a full humanity could become if it blossomed. What is missing is a national coordinated theological vision, a sober analysis, a life-giving spiritual presence, and a loose network that could help to create a new reality that would situate the bottom of society at the center of the country's top priorities. This vision would include both self-help projects inside the black community as well as pressure against governments, corporate entities, and other forces in civil society charged with the well-being of those at the bottom of the nation.

Black liberation theology must begin with the few prophetic churches, church-related institutions, and others who are struggling to offer leadership in African American communities and who take seriously a vocational calling to empower poor and other victims of dehumanizing structures. Black churches can play an important role because they make up perhaps the only national organization owned by the African American community. The chances of success for the church and black liberation theology to work with and on behalf of the least, the lost, and the left out in society greatly advance in partnership with womanist theology. Therefore, how might black liberation theology and womanist theology collaborate domestically and globally? How might they put in dialogue the second and third generations of each of their different traditions? What combination of new voices, odd and quirky voices, and radical and reformist voices might they introduce, and how does one map out the next twenty years? The value added of both theological communities exists in whether or not they make a difference in real lives. In the philosophical sense, both operate in the important world of ideas, while in the practical sense they realize that philosophers interpret the world in order to change it.

7

Womanist Gardens and Lies above Suspicion

Several dimensions of womanist studies in higher education and faith communities (i.e., churches, mosques, temples, shrines, and other ritual institutions) impact my way of developing theology as a second-generation black theologian.

Womanist sister scholars and faith leaders continue to propose the critical demand to keep liberation of and justice for the poor, the working class, and other marginalized communities at the center of all talk about God and gods. This proves a radical stance at the dawn of the twenty-first century. Now with the December 1991 dissolution of the Union of Soviet Socialist Republics (USSR) and the rise of the 1992 United States of America as the number-one global military power, it takes profound theoretical astuteness, deep faith commitments, loving compassion, and abundant courage to suggest an alternative and better world is possible. Contrastingly, most churches in the U.S. resume force-of-habit practices without heeding the prophetic calling to speak truth to power. In a word, Christian churches, in the main, continue a practice in support of what many black American womanists name as systems of patriarchy, heterosexism, white power, and monopoly capitalism.[1]

---

1. Keri Day, *Religious Resistance to Neoliberalism: Womanist and Black Feminist Perspectives* (New York: Palgrave Macmillan, 2015); Karen Baker-Fletcher, *Sisters of Dust, Sisters of Spirit: Womanist Wordings on God and Creation* (Minneapolis: Fortress, 1998); Kelly Brown Douglas, *The Black Christ*, The Bishop Henry McNeal Turner Studies in North American Black Religion 9 (Maryknoll, NY: Orbis, 1993); Cheryl A. Kirk-Duggan, *Exorcizing Evil: A Womanist Perspective on the Spirituals*, The Bishop Henry McNeal Turner/Sojourner Truth Studies in North American Black Religion 14 (Maryknoll, NY: Orbis, 1997); and Stacey Floyd-Thomas, *Mining the Motherlode: Methods in Womanist Ethics* (Cleveland: Pilgrim, 2006).

Likewise, the standard of European and European diaspora thought dominating the formal institutions of higher education in North America gives the surface appearance of denying that all education (whatever side one takes in the false debate between theology and religious studies) situates itself in support of systemic civic positions. But, in fact, one cannot breathe on earth and teach in U.S. schools and somehow produce so-called objective research detached from real people, institutions, and public policies. Every single theological school, seminary, divinity school and graduate religious studies program exists to support and promote the fundamental economic, political, military, and cultural way of life in the U.S. In fact, it is part of good citizenship and patriotic duty to stand with one's own country.

More specifically, as long as we black religious scholars pretend that we are individuals thinking on our own, that we have made it on our own, that it's chic to adopt the latest thought fad, that we have the right to detach from church and community movements, as long as we shy away from relying on the theories of our mothers and our fathers and the religious institutions that helped us get over, we remain minstrels for the cultures and structures of the white academy as it gives us exclusive back stage passes to our own black (white face?) performances.

This is when and where the womanists enter. They inspire my intellect. They weave a web of holism; an integrated vision of nondualism including, among other things, gender; class; race; sexual orientation; ecology; religious studies and theology together; faith and rigorous "objective" scholarship together; academy, church and community together; individual healing and radical transformation of U.S. structures and the artistic together.

Furthermore, *holism* in methodology and cosmology coupled with *faith* in a justice and liberation power beyond the human realm connect to their intentional *self-naming* as intergenerational African American women. We observe a sense of historical sweep and continuity among the womanists. That is why, for me, they self-consciously use the terms first-, second-, and third-generation womanist scholars. They teach me that structural and individual conversions in the United States will more likely result when black religious scholars work toward relating to previous scholars who put up the scaffolding for the house of our thought and practice. Contrary to this long view of the house that our parents and ancestors built, today's North American culture thrives on historical amnesia and instantaneous microwave individualism. But the womanists know where they come from and to whom they are linked.

Here too womanism cuts against the grain of people who believe they advance in the academy by themselves, by the brilliance of their individual intellect, and by the praises given them for being the first or only negro.

And, therefore, they feel that they are not part of anything and have the right to start their own "academic" trend or simply to clarify an "interesting" idea in one's head. It is a curious phenomenon that the black thinkers who pursue this path of "I have a right to think detached in the academy" actually are very communal. They submit to the marching orders of the European Enlightenment and command instructions from the majority of white scholars, who have created a culture and structure of this politically correct regime. The unannounced standard is that a person can act like he or she is thinking in the isolated womb of the academy without an umbilical cord to the outside world as long as the individual thinker does not challenge the ruling status quo in higher education.

More revealing perhaps is that the dominating voices (that is, the small group of true power brokers) in the academy self-consciously realize that the role of education in U.S. society is to propagate the dominant race and class in that society; as a citizen, one has loyalty to one's state. They know that this thing, at the plumb line foundation, is about the supremacy of elite European scholars and their diaspora. By definition, the U.S. academy, at its highest level, displays a preferential option for white patriarchal power, which goes against womanist knowledge.

Still, womanists show how to maneuver in institutions of higher education given unfair circumstances and one's own negativities and insecurities. They teach us that, yes, power resides in class formations and in between class structures. But at the same time, wherever domination rears its wicked community, possibilities for survival, quality of life, and resistance always exist. As long as we believe in a God who can take a crooked stick and hit a straight lick, and as long as we keep on keeping on, spiritual and material demons do not have the last word.

Consequently, womanists' theoretical work and their sheer bodily presence present ways of being joyful and affirming in education. They raise the bar of intellectual pursuits. This is what their (our) great-grandmothers and great-grandfathers did when they picked cotton; worked as domestics; owned businesses; entered industrial jobs; used Vaseline as a medicinal cure-all; conjured success out of segregated schools; became the first to get college degrees; broke into politics and exclusive professions; held our churches together; stayed with some black men too long; and worked successfully with red, brown, yellow, and white brothers and sisters. Their faith in God and the future of their grandchildren and great-grandchildren helped them to hold on and forge ahead even when they thought they could not hold on anymore. African American female scholars follow this same tradition when they quilt their being in the academy—take a little stitch of this and thread it with that and create a canopy that is big enough for all races and ethnic communities to get under and learn from. In this way, the institutions of higher education become locations for a vibrant give-and-take of ideas that matter.

In fact, the womanists are for power, but power from below, true democratic power and ownership by the majority. Such an innovative spiritual power and celebratory joy come from prior family generations and will prevail after we are long gone. It presents an old black folk wisdom saying that "man" didn't give it and "man" can't take it away. The power of a people originates from some Power greater than simply immediate earthly social arrangements. Such a foundational folk wisdom from spiritual power of black people's old-time religion contains centuries of everyday life lessons and tested theories of the people: God will fight your battles, but in the mean time you carry a Bible in one hand and defend yourself with the other, because God helps those who help themselves. I see this power blossoming in the mothers' gardens of womanists with their categorization of Alice Walker's four-part womanist definition: (1) radical subjectivity, (2) traditional communalism, (3) redemptive self-love, and (4) critical engagement. These four multicolored interpretations move my being to remain in the collective effort to press forward with antioppression, liberationist scholarship and practice.

In this chapter, womanist approaches move me to draw on the lies of African American folktales (that is, power from below) to pursue *holism* in methodology and cosmology coupled with *faith* in a justice and liberation Power beyond the human realm and to connect to an intentional *self-naming* as an intergenerational black theologian. I find a great part of my being here in these folk talks and in this heritage. And so for the rest of this chapter, as one way of learning from the womanist garden as well as my own mother's and grandmother's gardens in Richmond and rural Virginia, I will explore some lives above suspicion to discover being human in black folk talks. What can black people tell us (in higher education, church, and the broader public) about a sacred calling to be a healthy human being?

Lies for Being Human

One of the major forerunners for womanist thought and practice are the writings and life of Zora Neale Hurston, the daughter of a black Baptist preacher. Therefore, learning from both the gifts of womanist approaches in religion and society and the thought of Hurston, I'd like to advance the idea of "lies" from Hurston as a conceptual lens for constructing a contemporary definition of healthy being human. From 1928 to 1930, Hurston lived directly in research among the black working class and impoverished communities of Eatonville and Polk County, Florida as well as in New Orleans. The result is her original 1935 classic *Mules and Men*.[2] The theoretical beauty of these compiled and complicated folktales appears in their creating and revealing the positive self-referential nature of black folk's communal self.

In other words, neither a useless victim syndrome nor slavish subservience to white scholars, black folktales, here, blossom into radical subjectivity, traditional communalism, redemptive self-love, and critical practices. These stories or lies represent the world that blacks created, even though they are sane enough to recognize that white humanity does exist on earth. (In this regard, they symbolize the method of the creative genius of another pioneer of womanist wisdom, Toni Morison. Morison's brilliance continues to draw on the wealth of experiences primarily from black working peoples' own angelic and sinful natures.).

And so, to get at being human in black folktales, we have to plunge ourselves into the murky waters of some black lies. For instance, in a Florida community, Hurston runs across a group of black men congregated on a store porch. One fellow cries out, "Now you gointer hear lies above suspicion." Lies are stories or tales delivered with verbal skills. They present the art of living or how to be black in America. This intellectual and practical game requires cunning and flexibility. As another speaker demands of his colleagues, "We got plenty to do—lyin' . . . Lemme handle a li'l language long ere wid de rest."[3] Lies make a point with ethical importance and visions of the future for the human condition. Fact and fiction blend because the poor realize that truth incarnates in the folk who live out reality.

Four Models, Themes, and Spiritualities

The lies in black folktales offer us a flower garden of potentialities for a spiritually balanced and materially sharing humanity—that is, responses to the question: What has God created us to be, think, believe, say, and do in this world? At least four models come to mind: the *trickster* with the theme of *reversal* and a spirituality of *human flourishing*, the *conjurer* with the theme of *nature* and a spirituality of *all creation*, the *outlaw* with the theme of *ambiguity* and a spirituality of *individual desire*, and *Christian witness* with the theme of *empowerment* and a spirituality of *compassion for the poor*.

2. Zora Neale Hurston, *Mules and Men* (1935; reprint, Bloomington: Indiana University Press, 1978).

3. Both quotes are found respectively in ibid., 21 and 91.

The trickster character acts out the idea of reversal where usually the weak character uses the weapon of wit to outsmart the physically strong owners of material resources. His cunning produces a spirituality of human flourishing. Brer Rabbit is the main trickster character in this black folk paradigm. The Tar Baby lie, for example, shows Brer Rabbit constantly stealing water or crops from Brer Fox or Brer Wolf.[4]

Here the definition of human interaction means that the strongest should perform most of the work because they have monopolized most of the survival sustenance and technologies. Consequently, this unfair hoarding act has upset the balance of animal community harmony within the jungle or the woods. The weak, on the other hand, are called to see reality differently. They imagine creatively a vision of society in which the bottom levels have natural access to all that is healthy in life. The move to think, envision, and interpret from a more inclusive perspective empowers them to do whatever they need to do by using their instinctual mother wit and intentional intellect to overcome the incorrect circumstances created by the strong's focus on the individual self. Such reimagining helps a person to risk a new present in order to possess a better future. In the midst of terrible circumstances, entanglement in the tar of life, the weak look for hope.

After the trickster in African American folktales, conjure doctors are folk characters who call on elements from nature to perform either good or evil against another human being. Some claim that they receive the nature powers from association with the devil; others cite the grace of God's direct revelation. Still others point to their natural extraordinary gifts because they were born the seventh son of a seventh son with seven cauls covering their face; or another person swears on receiving wisdom passed down from the elderly long deceased.[5] At any rate, the conjurer introduces a spirituality of all creation.

---

4. Bruce Jackson, ed. *The Negro and His Folklore in Nineteenth-Century Periodicals*, Publications of the American Folklore Society. Bibliographical and Special Series 18 (Austin: University of Texas Press, 1967), 148–50. The article was taken from William Owens, "Folklore of the Southern Negro," *Lippincott's Magazine* 20 (Philadelphia, December 1877). Other versions of the Tar Baby cycle can be found in J. Mason Brewer, ed., *American Negro Folklore* (Chicago: Quadrangle, 1968), 7–9, originally published as "A Familiar Legend" in *The Hillsborough Recorder*, Hillsborough, NC, on August 5, 1874. Also, see Langston Hughes and Arna Bontemps, eds., *Book of Negro Folklore* (New York: Dodd, Mead, 1958), 1–2.

5. Leonara Herron and Alice M. Bacon, "Conjuring & Conjure-Doctors," in *Mother Wit from the Laughing Barrel: Readings in the Interpretation of Afro-American Folklore*, ed. Alan Dundes, Critical Studies on Black Life and Culture 7 (New York: Garland, 1981), 359–63. Reprinted from *Southern Workman* 24 (1895) 117–18, 193–94, 209–11. The stories in this article were collected in 1878.

Conjuring presents a humanity where equilibrium and disequilibrium are key for a comprehensive social interaction within culture. It stands as an aspect of theological anthropology (i.e., how humans imagine connections to their transcendent final goals to come) because it draws on human mystical ties to the supernatural powers crawling out from nature and from the strength of the spiritual (God or the devil) worlds. To be human, in the fullest sense imaginable, means learning from nature (i.e., animals, plants, air, water, and the earth).

Perhaps at first glance the third folk model, the outlaw character, appears as the most wicked model for what it means to be a healthy human self. Usually a male protagonist, this folk hero kills seemingly innocent bystanders, relates to women in a utilitarian manner, and, in general, creates chaos in community. Yet these surface aspects obscure the deeper appreciation that black working people and those living in structural poverty oftentimes generated from the ambiguity of outlaw or bad man toasts and ballads. The latter are created by and acknowledge a spirituality of human desire.

But despite the profound ambiguities of the outlaw (such as Shine and Stagolee), the community offers compassion even to seemingly misfits and potentially harmful characters. Where the larger culture disciplines (even to death) such folk figures, the tough love of the African American folk, in contrast, accepts them and thereby shows a certain practice of realistic and sober compassion. Here the model of "badness"—the outlaw—suggests a grey area (with a thin line between heroic acts and criminality) in the understanding of human nature.

The fourth and final model for theological anthropology (i.e., the spiritual and ethical dimensions of a new humanity) appears with the Christian witness causing empowerment and thereby producing a spirituality of compassion for the poor. Two historical figures speak to this model; and, though real persons, folklore legend has made them into superhuman, mythical people. Both Harriet Tubman and Denmark Vesey point to the revolutionary nature of prayer, a vocation of risks, the correlation of individual rights and privileges with the liberation of group status and communal empowerment, a biblical interpretation paralleling black folk with the oppressed ancient Israelite people, and global perspectives linking black Americans with the freedom of blacks worldwide.[6]

---

6. Sara Bradford, *Harriet Tubman: The Moses of Her People* (1868; reprint, Seacaucus, NJ: Citadel, 1961), 24–25, 84, and 29. John Oliver Killens, "Introduction," in *The Trial Record of Denmark Vesey* (Boston: Beacon, 1970), 70, 161, 64, 13, 42, 43, and 62.

A Christian Perspective on Being Human

As a Christian theologian (i.e., a conscious pursuer of the revelation of the Spirit of liberation through Jesus Christ with working-class people and those in structural poverty and consequently all of humanity), I am simultaneously informed by non-Christian theological anthropologies operating with a similar Spirit. In the four folk paradigms, I have discovered that a standard characteristic of God or an ultimate vision is a common search or journey on the part of the poor for communal life beyond monopoly capitalist restrictions. This Spirit of liberation (as well as a Spirit opposed to liberation) comes to the human condition and in human nature through different paths. Spirituality, therefore, is that which transcends the self, particularizes in a concrete but goes beyond a concrete, and carries positive and negative dimensions. Colaboring with God's Spirit, liberation becomes a move beyond harmful restrictions on the self and the poor and, as a result, a pointer to freedom practice.

Freedom, as a result, is to love the creative humanity of the poor as God loves the poor. This reveals the *imago dei* (i.e., image of God) incarnated in real flesh. It stands for human efforts to open up space for those once chained internally by psychological sin and externally by structural sin. More specifically, the first aspect of the image of God means awareness of who we are as human beings—imaging God by creating healthy life without restrictions and collectively owning all wealth on earth.

In conjunction with knowing who you are, being made in God's image is accompanied by a second aspect—knowing whose you are. Filled with knowledge of whose you are, one knows that she is possessed by a spiritual calling to subordinate oneself to the service of others. Jesus walked this earth with that purpose in life.

Freedom, furthermore, grows beyond acceptance of one's *imago dei* (i.e., image of God). A holding pattern of mere acceptance eventually harms the Spirit's gift of God's image. Rather, the divinity works with us and loves us into carrying out this good news. In other words, the *imago dei* unfolds outward into the *missio dei* (i.e., the mission of God to the world). We are called to practice healthy humanity by recognizing the divine image in others and sharing this liberation evangelism for others' freedom. And the four models aid us to put more flesh on the bones of what we mean by freedom.

The Christian witness and empowerment give us a spirituality of compassion for and service with the poor. These types of lies show us a spirituality that requires a self-love; love of others, including the stranger; love of God; and a love, based on justice, of the oppressor. The conjurer with nature teaches us about a spirituality of all creation. We, therefore, need to be attentive to revelation of power in directions (i.e., north, south, east, and west), elements (i.e., air, water, dirt, and fire), animals and plants, and time dimensions. The outlaw with ambiguity gifts us with a spirituality of individual desire urging our direct assertion of our unique identities, space, and voices. Individual desire accepts sensuality and sexuality of the body, where one also finds the attached brain. Finally, the trickster and reversal means a spirituality of human flourishing leading to innovation, cunning, and balance.

So my response to womanists' gardens, and their impact on religion and society, emphasizes and highlights their stress on the voices of the margins, those from below. In the lies above suspicion in black folktales, I discover a sacred healthy human being creating a new family composed of people, nature, and the cosmos, a gathering of hopeful energy for everything that points toward the joyful and innovative sense of a better world is possible—of course, grounded primarily in right relations of spiritual balance and material justice among all of the created order.

8

Enslaved Black Women: A Theology of Justice and Reparations[1]

Introduction

Many black women who had been enslaved in the United States never doubted that their God would do right where others had done wrong. They believed that God would not allow the great suffering of black women's bodies and minds to go unanswered. Some type of restitution and reparations were in order. After the hell of the Civil War (1865), Mrs. Lucy Delaney exclaimed, "Slavery! Cursed slavery! What crimes has it invoked! And, oh! What retribution has a righteous God visited upon these traders in human flesh!"[2]

Mrs. Maria W. Stewart showed similar confidence in her God's justice in her 1834 autobiography. She wailed against America's "foul and indelible stain" and declared this a nation marked "for thy cruel wrongs and injuries to the fallen sons [and daughters] of Africa." God, she wrote, would plead the case of the oppressed against the oppressor and would provide "charity," even if it were a "small return" for the suffering of black women and men. Giving evidence in her argument for reparations, Mrs. Stewart asserted, "We will tell you, that it is our gold that clothes you in fine linen and purple, and causes you to fare sumptuously every day; and it is the blood of our

---

1. I am appreciative of Jill Hazelton for suggesting improvements in the outline of this essay.

2. Lucy Delaney, "From the Darkness Cometh the Light, or, Struggles for Freedom," in *Six Women's Slave Narratives*, Schomburg Library of Nineteenth-Century Black Women Writers (1857; reprint, New York: Oxford University Press, 1988), 14.

fathers, and the tears of our brethren that have enriched your soils. AND WE CLAIM OUR RIGHTS."[3]

Some decades after the Civil War, Mrs. Callie House led a movement of more than three hundred thousand ex-slaves to petition the government to pay them pensions for their labor. Mrs. House organized through churches, including her own, the Primitive Baptist, which was largely composed of poor people. Mrs. House, who did heavy manual labor as a washerwoman in Nashville, stated in 1899, "My Whole Soul and body are for this ex-slave movement and are willing to sacrifice for it." Indeed, Mrs. House was imprisoned for "fraudulently" giving the hope of an old-age pension to ex-slaves.[4]

These faith testimonies and the nation's history urge us to rethink the relationship between the need to repair the effects of slavery, on the one hand, and ideas about collective responsibility, on the other. The process of considering rights and responsibilities regarding reparations for slavery might help restore the material and spiritual health of America.

But many Americans today deny that they are reaping benefits from the past system of slavery. They perceive no connection between their lives and the need to restore justice for today's black women based on wrongs during the period when Americans owned other humans as chattel. Yet Americans belong to a nation that codified and practiced the trade in black human flesh and prospers from it to this day.

A variety of arguments are offered against the payment of restitution (returning something lost or stolen) or reparations (making amends for doing wrong) for slavery:[5]

1. "Since slavery ended quite some time ago, the nation should get over it and move on." In fact, the nation's legacy of injustice continues to play out in its economic system and in the spiritual makeup of its people.

2. "My family did not own slaves." This may be true. The issue, however, is not one of tracing connections to past individual slaveholders. Rather, the issue is recognizing the system of disproportionate benefits given

---

3. Maria W. Stewart, "Productions of Mrs. Maria W. Stewart Presented to the First African Baptist Church & Society of the City of Boston," in *Spiritual Narratives*, Schomburg Library of Nineteenth-Century Black Women Writers (1835; reprint, New York: Oxford University Press, 1988), 17–21.

4. See Mary Frances Berry, *My Face Is Black Is True: Callie House and the Struggle for Ex-Slave Reparations* (New York: Knopf, 2005), 7, 212.

5. For more on these and other arguments, see Christopher Hitchens, "Debt of Honor," in *Should America Pay? Slavery and the Raging Debate on Reparations*, ed. Raymond A. Winbush (New York: HarperCollins, 2003), 172–79; and Molly Secours, "Riding the Reparations Bandwagon," in *Should America Pay?*, 286–98, 399.

to some U.S. citizens and denied to others as a direct and immediate result of the U.S. slavery system.

3. "African Americans already have privileges manifested in affirmative action programs." In fact, these programs affect very small numbers of people. They have not benefited the majority of blacks, who are working-class, nonprofessional, and working-poor people.

4. "I don't believe in white superiority." Again, the issue is the responsibility of our society as a whole and the fact that whatever one's beliefs, too many white citizens continue to benefit from the wealth that whites get from uncompensated black labor during the slavery era.

5. "Reparations will divide blacks and whites." But blacks and whites are already divided; wealth, income, residential, job, health, education, and other indicators of well-being all show a racial hierarchy and disparity. The playing field is not level.

While aware of these concerns, in this chapter I lay out how the faith commitments of Mrs. Delaney, Mrs. Stewart, and Mrs. House can hint at ways to move beyond our slaveholding legacy to establish the more just order that they imagined. Creating just relations among people and within institutions requires rectifying past wrongs and the persistent racial and gender discrimination that grows from them. The route to rectification involves producing healthy individuals and public policy and a reconstructed economic system. Taking the faith of these women seriously is a first step along that path.

I argue that a more just order has to include restorative justice, a type of reparations that I advocate in this chapter. Restorative justice begins with an apology from the wrongdoer. In the case of American slavery, this means the government and corporations, a process that has begun with the apology for slavery issued by the House of Representatives in 2008.[6] Public apology soothes the spiritual hurt of the abused. And the apology helps the oppressor group to start lifting its burden of guilt. In addition, restorative justice requires listening to the victims of the crimes, trauma, or sin at issue; hearing their stories; and working with the forms of repair that they suggest. Finally, the victims' statements of forgiveness relieve the guilty party of guilt.

In restorative justice, both parties take on active, interactive roles. The perpetrator speaks an apology. The victim accepts the apology or at

---

6. *Apologizing for the Enslavement and Racial Segregation of African-Americans*, HR 194, 110th Cong., 2nd sess., *Congressional Record* 154, no. 127, daily ed. (July 29, 2008): H 7224.

least enters into dialogue. The advantaged group hears the case of the disadvantaged. The wrongdoer repairs the relationship by providing material compensation for the wrong. The victim advances more forgiveness. Community is formed through restoring justice with forgiveness and reconciliation. Both parties experience healing through their words and actions.

Ultimately, restoring justice to the victims helps the rebuilding of better relations among all parties, both the perpetrators and the injured petitioners for relief. At its root, restorative justice brings material and spiritual healing; that is, it involves caring for the whole person and the entire nation.[7] With healthy individual and corporate bodies, reconciliation follows. From a theological perspective, restorative justice means healing, forgiveness, and community.

Theology, in the context of restorative justice, explains how people understand their situation in relation to faith in a divinity who heals the broken hearted and heals shattered systems. Mrs. Delaney, Mrs. Stewart, Mrs. House, and many other enslaved and formerly enslaved black Americans knew that God would always take care of the victims and make things right. Their faith provides a conceptual framework for thinking about the possibility of reparations.

During the great suffering of slavery, enslaved African and African American women were not paid for laboring in the Big House, in the fields, and in their own slave shacks. No one compensated them for serving as the objects of white male lust. And they have not received restitution for the physical or psychological trauma of their transgenerational suffering. From roughly 1441 (when the first group of enslaved Africans were taken to Portugal) to 1865 (the end of the Civil War), black women were forced to surrender their bodies and their families to the whites who owned them. As a result, a small group of elite men of one race accumulated unmerited, unearned wealth. They passed that wealth down to their sons and, to a lesser degree, daughters, who also handed it on down through the generations. This tradition contrasts with the tradition enslaved African American women left to their children, one that includes rage, shame, pride, and a fierce belief in justice. Although wealth brought numerous opportunities to the white descendants of slaveholders, lack of wealth continues to plague the descendants of the enslaved.

Progressive Christians understand that the actions of the community's members affect the rest of the community across time and space. These Christians, who feel connected with other Christians both past and present,

---

7. See Mark S. Umbreit, "Restorative Justice in the Twenty-First Century: A Social Movement Full of Opportunities and Pitfalls," *Marquette University Law Review* 89 (2005) 251.

want to atone for the past wrongs of Christian slaveholders. And they want to practice the calls of enslaved Christians from the past for some form of reparations. Christians in the United States can draw on the experiences of Mrs. Stewart, Mrs. Delaney, Mrs. House, and their sisters and cousins, and mothers and daughters, to explore theologically how to reduce the long-term damage of slavery by creating just policies in the present.

Theology and Justice

The reasons for considering theology and justice together might not be obvious the first time. Many people—including many theologians—see Christianity mainly as offering a spiritual resolution to the material world's predicaments. That is, they think that there are two realms: a secular realm, which is this world, and a spiritual realm, which is God's realm. They see Jesus Christ's pure world as antagonistic to the sinful affairs of the earth. They think of sin mainly as personal and individual missteps on the part of individual women and men. One should not lie, steal, fornicate, curse, and so forth. In this way of thinking, sin consists of the multiple individual errors of each person on the globe. All have fallen short of God's justice and law. Therefore, sins that groups of people build into their societies, such as slavery, do not register as sins because there is no category for sins by a group. Many, or even most, nineteenth-century white Christians saw no sin in slavery. In this view, it would not be sinful to worship in a church built by enslaved persons or to hold stock in a transportation company using tracks laid by enslaved workers. This breaking of life into spiritual and material realms is typical of the conservative theology of many Pentecostal, charismatic, and prosperity-gospel preachers.

Liberal and mainstream theology also does not give us an adequate mission to form a more just society. Such church people as the Episcopalians, Presbyterians, United Methodists, and Roman Catholics believe in the concept of social sin. They correctly highlight social justice in God's created world. But the uncontrolled individualism of American culture creates a counterweight to this acknowledgment of social sin, with the result that these same Christians do not feel responsible unless they have directly participated in society's wrongdoing. Thus, these theologies do not deal adequately with the structures of racism or with the ways in which slavery allowed whites to accumulate wealth for free because both of these problems originated in the past and not the present. Considering the idea of social justice missing in these theologies, Sheila Briggs observes: "Social justice requires that we take responsibility not only for our own actions, but also for those of our communities. Since communities continue over time, then this responsibility is not just for what happens during our individual lifetime, but is trans-historical and therefore must address the consequences of slavery, because they have survived with our communities."[8]

Summing up my perspective thus far, it is clear that both the two-realms theology and the theology of personal responsibility overshadowing communal obligations lack a fundamental definition of justice as collective accountability. They do not help us understand how to address the past, present, and persistent inequities of the American slavery system.

Human accountability, including accountability for our social structures, is central to theology. Theology is, in fact, an accountability discipline. The word *theology* comes from two Greek words: *theos*, which means "God," and *logos*, which means "word" or "reason." Theologians ask questions about God and about the interaction between God and human beings. Are humans faithful to God? What is the faith to which God has called them? Do their actions reflect that faith? Theologians are also constantly adapting Christian tradition to present circumstances. Theology challenges Christians to live by what they believe and points them toward a faith that addresses the pressing moral issues of the day. The unfinished business of slavery is a pressing moral challenge for our day. We can learn to address this opportunity by remembering the faith of enslaved black women who understood that faith must include justice.

Black Women's Experience

Enslaved black women's theology differed from that of their slave masters not only because they disagreed ideologically. Enslaved African American women believed differently because their material life circumstances contrasted so greatly with those of their owners. The sins of life as these women experienced them called for the implementation of justice in the material world, if not for enslaved women, then for their generations to come. Divine justice lacks legal limits of time and space. The theology of a God who created nature for all humans to share arises out of the concrete circumstances of enslaved black women's earthly plight and prospects. A theological basis for reparations for black women thus requires an investigation of what these women gave and what they did not receive.

The unpaid labor of African women, and subsequently African American women, starts with their capture on the west coast of Africa.[9] This vi-

8. This comes from e-mail correspondence with Sheila Briggs on April 2, 2008.

9. Native Americans were also enslaved in the colonies and the United States, and

cious encounter began the white redefinition of these women's identities to serve the needs of their owners. From the time they were abducted, sold, or traded into the European Christian slave system, their owners used these women as (1) laborers, (2) reproducers of laborers, and (3) sexual objects of white male lust.

African women, along with men, were sold or traded to white businessmen who usually waited for their arrival on the Atlantic coast of Africa. Adventuresome white men carried out direct attacks on African communities. In some cases, white entrepreneurs paid African clans to capture other language groups, bought Africans who were already prisoners or war, or otherwise applied divide-and-conquer tactics among African peoples.[10]

The first experience of African women reduced to slavery was the trauma of being captured by force and removed from family, familiar surroundings, the faith of the clan, and the fun memories of being safe and loved. Then came the grueling days of walking from the interior to the sea in what were called caravans. Many died along the way.

On the shore, the second part of their becoming exiles from Africa unfolded. They were housed in small, crowded shacks called barracoons, or they were put underground in slave castles. More deaths, the stench of body waste, the lack of food and water, and rape by white men became routine.

After weeks in stifling heat and inhuman living conditions on the coast, the months-long final leg of their forced exile began for these women; they were herded aboard slave ships headed for the Caribbean or South and North America. On the sea, African women experienced cruel rituals of rape at the hands of crewmen and European adventurers. Impregnated women were already carrying future laborers for the system of bondage that waited for them in the so-called New World.

---

small numbers of Native Americans and African Americans are known to have owned slaves. This analysis focuses on the experiences of African American women owned by whites as most typical of plantation-system slavery in the United States.

10. References for the following paragraphs: Darlene Clark Hine and Kathleen Thompson, *A Shining Thread of Hope: The History of Black Women in America* (New York: Broadway, 1998); Angela Yvonne Davis, *Women, Race, & Class* (New York: Vintage, 1983); Jacqueline Jones, *Labor of Love, Labor of Sorrow: Black Women, Work, Family from Slavery to the Present* (New York: Vintage, 1986); William St. Clair, *The Door of No Return: The History of the Cape Coast Castle and the Atlantic Slave Trade* (New York: BlueBridge, 2007); David E. Stannard, *American Holocaust: The Conquest of the New World* (New York: Oxford University Press, 1992); and Robin Blackburn, *The Making of New World Slavery: From the Baroque to the Modern, 1492–1800* (London: Verso, 1997). For the complicity of some Africans in the European Christian slave trade, see Saidiya Hartman, *Lose Your Mother: A Journey Along the Atlantic Slave Route* (New York: Farrar, Straus & Giroux, 2008).

When the ships arrived, the surviving Africans were not necessarily sold immediately. Some prospective buyers came out to the ships to examine women's breasts and reproductive areas to discover their productivity and reproductivity. African women (and men) might remain in cramped ship's quarters for weeks awaiting sale. Even when Africans were unloaded from the ships (with names like *Jesus*, *Mary*, and *Brotherhood*) and dragged ashore, they might be kept in coastal dungeons so prospective buyers could consider their reproductive capabilities. The eventual purchase of these captured Africans meant they had to walk miles, hours, and days to their new shacks on slave plantations. Along the way, some died, exhausted from traveling on foot.

Forced Labor

Enslaved African and African American women labored without pay so that a small group of elite white men could accumulate wealth and pass it on to their descendants. Owners of plantations and factories gained immense unearned profits from several centuries of unpaid African and African American labor. Black women worked as house slaves around the master, mistress, and their children. They worked in the field performing the same duties as black men. And they toiled at night carrying out chores for their own enslaved family. All three forms of uncompensated labor produced free wealth accumulation for white men and their families.

Housework began at an early age for girls. Several former enslaved women remembered this process: "When I was about six years old they take me into the big house to learn to be a house woman, and they show me how to cook and clean up and take care of babies . . . help the cooks and peel the potatoes and pick the guineas and chickens . . . I had to get up way before daylight and make the fire in the kitchen fireplace and bring in some fresh water, and go get the milk."[11] After these elaborate preparations performed by a six-year-old baby-child, then "Old Master and Old Mistress" came in for breakfast. The little girl's next job was to stand silently behind her white owners and shoo off the flies while her owners enjoyed a full meal.

Another former enslaved elderly woman remembers, "When I was nine years old, dey took me from my mother an' sol' me." Furthermore, she tells how "Massa Tinsely made me de house girl." Jobs incuded making beds, cleaning the house, standing quietly in the mistress's room until she noticed the nine-year-old, lowering the shades throughout the house, filling

---

11. Dorothy Sterling, ed., *We Are Your Sisters: Black Women in the Nineteenth Century* (New York: Norton, 1984), 7.

water pitchers, and arranging towels on wash stands. The child was not allowed to ever sit down, especially in the presence of white people.[12]

Older women participated in more sustained work. Some wove thread into cloth to make clothes and blankets for the plantation owner. After the weaving was done, slaves took the materials to the dyeing room where another black woman, knowledgeable in roots, leaves, barks, and berries, brought to the cloth the colors of the rainbow. The final stage in this use of African American women's labor with clothing was sewing the dyed cloth into the items demanded by the slave master.[13]

And then there was the cooking. White families enjoyed the luxury of not having to grow, harvest, prepare, cook, or serve food to themselves. Black women worked hard in the kitchen all day to produce meals for others. Black women grew the fruits and vegetables, nurtured and then slaughtered the livestock, and milked the cows. After fetching the firewood, they prepared a scrumptious meal for the plantation owners.[14]

Enslaved women also worked in the fields. In the Southern economy, slaves and land ownership were the two major sources of white wealth until the Civil War.[15] Forced fieldwork was even assigned to little girls. The testimony of formerly enslaved women explains these chores. "When I was a little bitty girl dey used to make a scarecrow outen me. Dey'd make me git up fo' daybreak an' go out into de cornfields an' set dere till way pas dark . . ." Another youngster was the "gap tender," that is, the one who opened and closed fence gates, called gaps, so that white people could walk and ride through any time of the day. In contrast to her having to stand all day controlling the gate, she describes the freedom of movement of farm animals: "De cattle am 'lowed to run where dey wants, here, there and all over." Children worked in groups when it came to "pickin' de bugs off de terbaccy leaves." And a very small child was forced to work with a hoe in order to scrape cornfields.[16]

---

12. Ibid. See also George P. Rawick, ed., *The American Slave: A Composite Autobiography: Supplement*, Series 1, vol. 6, *Alabama Narratives* (Westport, CT: Greenwood, 1978), 183; and Rawick, ed., *The American Slave*, vol. 7, *Mississippi Narratives, Part 2*, 400. See also Patricia Hill Collins, *Black Feminist Thought: Knowledge, Consciousness, and the Politics of Empowerment*, rev. 10th ann. ed. (New York: Routledge, 2000), 46–52.

13. Sterling, *We Are Your Sisters*, 17; and Deborah Gray White, *Ar'n't I a Woman? Female Slaves in the Plantation South* (New York: Norton, 1985), 115.

14. See also Gerda Lerner, ed., *Black Women in White America: A Documentary History* (New York: Vintage, 1973), 17–22.

15. Claud Anderson, *Black Labor, White Wealth: The Search for Power and Economic Justice* (Edgewood, MD: Duncan & Duncan, 1994), 133–34.

16. Quoted in Sterling, *We Are Your Sisters*, 8.

Adult women were expected to work as hard as grown men. "I split rails like a man," said one former enslaved woman. Others echoed her experience. "I drive the gin, what was run by two mules." And in these words: "My mama could hunt good as any man." Another exclaimed, "I toted bricks ... I fired de furnace..."[17] Women repaired roads, rolled and cut logs, set rail fences, fed chickens and pigs, and took care of the horses on the plantation.

Enslaved African American women worked alongside men in the rice fields of South Carolina, on tobacco plantations in Virginia, and in sugarcane fields in Louisiana. Cotton became king in Dixie with the 1793 invention of the cotton gin, a mechanical device removing seeds from the raw cotton. Women participated in every phase of the cotton production process. They "plowed fields; dropped seed; and hoed, picked, ginned, sorted, and moted cotton." Though picking 120 to two hundred pounds of cotton a day indicated a good average worker's ability, some women doubled that amount, picking four hundred to five hundred pounds per day. Even while pregnant, black women were forced, under penalty of the whip, to pick cotton.[18] The coldest months of cotton picking, like January, saw them working with frostbitten and bleeding hands and feet.

Enslaved women also labored in businesses linked to the growing industrial Southern economy. They were ditch diggers and lumberjacks. They worked in iron foundries and coal mines, where they replaced animals pulling trams in Southern mines. They were 50 percent of the workforce that produced the Santee Canal in South Carolina. They labored on Louisiana levees and helped build Southern railroads still used today.[19]

After a day of heavy labor, enslaved black women further enriched their owners by returning to their own slave homes to prepare their family to return the next morning to work for the slave master. Late at night in a slave shack, they mended clothes; cooked their meager meals; helped the sick; made soap and candles; grew, preserved, and stored food; dyed thread and wove cloth to make clothes; churned butter; conjured natural home remedies for wounds and illnesses; and heard the reports of emotional and physical pain felt by their children and husbands.

---

17. Quoted in ibid., 13.

18. Jacqueline Jones, *Labor of Love, Labor of Sorrow: Black Women, Work, Family from Slavery to the Present* (New York: Vintage, 1986), 15–18.

19. Angela Yvonne Davis, *Women, Race, & Class* (New York: Vintage, 1983), 10.

The Body as Producer of Wealth

Plantation owners saw the bodies of black women as machines for producing more workers who could be sold to the highest bidder at the slave markets on Wall Street or in Charleston, South Carolina, or who could remain as laborers on the estate where the black person was born. Both circumstances produced income and wealth for the white owner. "Breeders" were enslaved women set aside to be impregnated by both white and black men in order to birth laborers at no cost to their owners.[20]

This view of black women's bodies as machines for the creation of wealth was not the exception or unplanned practice of a few white landowners. Quite the contrary, state and local governments institutionalized the subordination of black women's reproduction through legislation.[21] Early on, when the first group of a little more than three women, along with about seventeen men, was brought to Jamestown, Virginia, in August 1619, some African women began to lose their reproductive rights. In 1662, the Jamestown legislature declared all children born of enslaved black women to be enslaved.

Despite the laws they made against miscegenation, plantation owners used African and African American women's bodies whenever the men chose to satisfy their lust for sex, for power, and for the creation of property. They practiced at least three forms of sexual injustice: (1) they exercised their privileged white male right to black women's bodies, (2) they chose husbands for black women, and (3) they rented black men out as studs to impregnate black women.

Formerly enslaved women remembered clearly the first form of sexual injustice. Mrs. Savilla Burrell reported, "Old Marster was the daddy of some mulatto children." Other plantation owners segregated black women to use for sex. Any man could visit the segregated group to rape a black woman and then go about his business. Mrs. Mattie Curtis recalled, "Mr. Mordicia [the slave master] had his yeller gals in one quarter to themselves and these gals belong to the Mordicia men, their friends, and the overseers. When a baby was born in that quarter, they'd send it over to the black quarter at birth." When a girl baby was produced, she grew up and was sent back to

---

20. Ibid., 7.

21. For example, see in this volume Fay Botham, "The 'Purity of the White Woman, not the Purity of the Negro Woman': The Contemporary Legacies of Historical Laws against Interracial Marriage"; and Catherine Clinton, "Breaking the Silence: Sexual Hypocrisies from Thomas Jefferson to Strom Thurmond." See also Pamela Bridgewater, "Ain't I a Slave: Slavery, Reproductive Abuses and Reparations," *UCLA Women's Law Journal* 14 (2005).

the light-skinned women's quarters, where she "had more children for her daddy or brother."[22] Those children counted as free wealth, expanding their master's holdings.

Other men performed a ritual of gang rape on little girls. A formerly enslaved woman retells the history of her sister during chattel days: "My sister was given away when she was a girl. She told me and ma that they'd make her go out and lay on a table and two or three white men would have sex with her before they'd let her up. She was just a small girl. She died when she was still in her young days, still a girl."[23] Christian plantation owners and their white wives aped the powers of God by deciding which black men enslaved African American women could marry or live with. Mrs. Hilliard Yellerday, a survivor of slavery days, retold her memory of this customary practice: "Some of them [black women] had children at the age of twelve and thirteen years old. Negro men six feet tall went to some of these children."[24] One mistress gave her servant direct orders about whom to have babies with and whom not to: "Don't you ever let me see you with that ape again," threatened the mistress. "If you cannot pick a mate better than that I'll do the picking for you."[25]

Beyond free access to black women's bodies and forced partnering, plantation owners also institutionalized breeding to create a future enslaved workforce that was tall and strong. Owners hired out enslaved black men like bulls to stud black women on other plantations. An ex-slave testifies, "Dey uster take women away fum dere husbands an' put wid some other man to breed jes' like dey would do cattle." And just as prize bulls carried out a daily routine of fathering offspring, so too did black men function as basic sperm donors: "Dey always kept a man penned up an' dey used im' like a stud hoss."[26] These various forms of forced reproduction created wealth for white owners. Mrs. Tempie Herndon knew well her value to her master: "I was worth a heap to Marse George 'cause I had so many chillen. De more chillen a slave had de more dey was worth."[27]

Finally, light-skinned black women earned a premium for their owners when sold to businesses in such commercial centers as New Orleans. The so-called fancy trade was an exclusive market for white men who traveled

---

22. Quoted in Darlene Clark Hine and Kathleen Thompson, *A Shining Thread of Hope: The History of Black Women in America* (New York: Broadway, 1998), 98.

23. Quoted in Dorothy Sterling, ed., *We Are Your Sisters*, 25.

24. Quoted in Hine and Thompson, *Shining Thread of Hope*, 80.

25. Quoted in Jacqueline Jones, *Labor of Love, Labor of Sorrow*, 34.

26. Dwight N. Hopkins, *Down, Up, and Over: Slave Religion and Black Theology* (Minneapolis: Fortress, 1999), 63.

27. Quoted in Sterling, ed., *We Are Your Sisters*, 31.

to New Orleans, Charleston, St. Louis, or Lexington to purchase women of varying colors (mulatto, quadroon, octoroon) to use as prostitutes or concubines. The sexual violence of their white fathers, grandfathers, and great-grandfathers made these women vulnerable to continued trauma caused by requiring them to submit sexually to white men.[28]

Enslaved African American women were not only physically abused. They suffered psychological abuse as well. Black mothers had no choice but to watch the sale of their children in slave markets up and down the Eastern Seaboard.[29] "Babies was snatched from deir mother's breasts and sold to speculators," stated one former female slave. Another remembered how the master and a speculator (the slave buyer) walked among enslaved black people working in the fields. When the African Americans were together eating later that night, a mother looked frantically among the slaves who had returned from the field. Not seeing her child, she knew the white master had sold him. She exclaimed: "'De speculator, de speculator.' Den de tears roll down her cheeks, cause maybe it her son or husband and she knows she never see em again."[30] Another master, who had just sold a black woman's child, told her, "'Stop that sniffing there if you don't want to get a whipping.'"[31]

Slave masters also created stereotypes of black women in order to justify their inhuman treatment and to wear down their self-esteem. The damage done by these stereotypes continues to dog our society to this day.[32]

One deceptive stereotype is the Mammy character. In the white imagination, Mammy was asexual, a female lacking the natural libido of healthy women. This overweight, maternal martyr ran the Big House of the master and sacrificed herself day and night to maintain order and discipline in the cooking and cleaning, the administration of house affairs, and the compassionate nurturing, protection, and rearing of white children. Mammy was a superwoman. She was trustworthy, respectful, and loyal; some even called

---

28. White, *Ar'n't I a Woman?* 37.

29. Pamela Bridgewater, "Ain't I a Slave: Slavery, Reproductive Abuses and Reparations," *UCLA Women's Law Journal* 14 (2005).

30. Quotes are from Sterling, ed., *We Are Your Sisters* (New York: Norton, 1984), 10, 43, respectively.

31. Quoted in Hine and Thompson, *Shining Thread of Hope*, 98.

32. See Frances Smith Foster, "Mammy's Daughters; Or, the DNA of a Feminist Sexual Ethics," in *Beyond Slavery: Overcoming Its Religious and Sexual Legacies*, ed. Bernadette J. Brooten and Jaqueline L. Hazelton (New York: Palgrave Macmillan, 2010), 267–84; Dorothy Roberts, "The Paradox of Silence and Display: Sexual Violation of Enslaved Women and Contemporary Contradictions in Black Female Sexuality," in ibid., 41–60; and Emilie M. Townes, "From Mammy to Welfare Queen: Images of Black Women in PublicPolicy Formation," in ibid., 61–74.

her an aristocrat. In reality, this white psychological projection undercut black women's self-esteem by making their actual lives invisible.[33]

If the Mammy myth was of the asexual woman, the opposite extreme in the denial of the reality of the lives of enslaved black women was the lie of the Jezebel. Jezebel, the ultimate temptress, woke up each day and schemed to have uncontrollable sex. Her life's purpose was fulfilling the sexual fantasies and desires of white men. Mammy led men to heaven. Jezebel led them to hell. Mammy lacked libido. Jezebel overflowed with the libido. White men and their women described Jezebel as lewd, addicted to the pleasures of the flesh, and eaten by wild lust. Her body burned in constant need of a man. The myth became so powerful that some slave masters placed newspaper ads describing their enslaved women as able to please any man by night and by day because of their fiery and promiscuous nature.[34]

Slavery's Legacy and Black Women's Theology

Black women's enslaved experiences provide a factual basis for developing a theology of justice through reparations. In addition, the legacy of wealth accumulation during slavery has created huge discrepancies between contemporary whites and blacks, especially African American women, increasing the need for a theology of justice that involves reparations.

Wealth is not only income, or a paycheck. Inherited wealth passed down through generations in white families is the key to the reparations owed to black women. Indeed, inherited wealth in the white community is the basis of contemporary black-white inequality.

Wealth means economic assets, including pension funds, houses and other real estate, works of art, businesses, cars, cash, and stocks and bonds. Wealth includes land, natural resources, commercial buildings, trust funds, "down payments and closing costs for first-time homebuyers, college tuition, large cash gifts, and loans, as well as old-fashioned bequests at death."[35] Wealth is also home equity, savings accounts, silver, and antiques. One has wealth when one owns and controls capital and resources. One has

---

33. White, *Ar'n't I a Woman?*, 45-56.

34. Ibid., 29-32. See also Yanick St. Jean and Joe R. Feagin, *Double Burden: Black Women and Everyday Racism* (Armonk, NY: Sharpe, 1999), 5-15 and 100-105; and Collins, *Black Feminist Thought*, 72-75, 81-84.

35. Thomas M. Shapiro, *The Hidden Cost of Being African American: How Wealth Perpetuates Inequality* (New York: Oxford University Press, 2004), 10-11.

income when one gets a salary or works for someone else. Wealth provides opportunities, including the ability to pass wealth along to one's children.[36]

The net worth of our parents, grandparents, and earlier generations heavily influences wealth because most private wealth in the United States is inherited.[37] Whites, especially the richest families, have accumulated wealth through inheritance, generation after generation. African Americans have not seen growth in their net assets. In 1865, the year the Civil War ended, blacks owned 0.5 percent of all U.S. wealth. In 1990, they owned 1 percent. Virtually no progress has taken place.[38]

American wealth is concentrated in very few hands. Since the days of the European and European American Christian slave trade, 80 percent of family wealth has come through inheritance, not individual savings.[39] The wealthiest 1 percent of families owns 47 percent of America's financial wealth (businesses, real estate, buildings, other financial instruments, stocks, and bonds), and the United States continues to undergo a redistribution of wealth upward.[40] According to a study by the U.S. Federal Reserve, as of 2007 the typical African American family held ten cents in wealth for every dollar held by the typical white family. That is a decline from 2004, when the typical African American family had twelve cents in wealth for every dollar held by a white family.[41] At every income level, white households have significantly higher median wealth than black households earning similar amounts of money. At the highest income level, white net worth is $133,607, compared to $43,806 for blacks. At the lowest income level, net worth for typical white households is $17,066, compared to $2,400 for black households.[42] Among women, white widows have more than $15,000 in assets on average, but black widows have no assets.[43] A 2006 study found that white female heads of household earn an average of $13,202 annually

---

36. Melvin L. Oliver and Thomas M. Shapiro, *Black Wealth, White Wealth: A New Perspective on Racial Inequality*, 10th ann. ed. (New York: Routledge, 2006), 2, 203.

37. Meizhu Lui et al., *The Color of Wealth: The Story behind the U.S. Racial Wealth Divide* (New York: New Press, 2006), 2. Also review Dalton Conley, *Being Black, Living in the Red: Race, Wealth, and Social Policy in America* (Berkeley: University of California Press, 1999), 5 and 10–11; and Claud Anderson, *Black Labor–White Wealth: The Search for Power and Economic Justice* (Bethesda, MD: PowerNomics, 1994).

38. Conley, *Being Black*, 25.

39. Shapiro, *Hidden Cost*, 61; and Lui, *Color of Wealth*, 8.

40. Oliver and Shapiro, *Black Wealth, White Wealth*, 201; and Shapiro, *Hidden Cost*, 44. On the wealth-redistribution figures, see Lui, *Color of Wealth*, 13.

41. Meizhu Lui, "The Wealth Gap Gets Wider," Op-Ed, *Washington Post*, March 23, 2009.

42. Shapiro, *The Hidden Cost*, 47–49.

43. Oliver and Shapiro, *Black Wealth, White Wealth*, 126.

and have $23,530 in net worth, compared to $10,245 earned on average annually by black female heads of household, who have a net worth of $500 on average.[44]

After slavery, the U.S. government and individuals continued to increase the development of white wealth and to cripple the creation of black wealth. The Southern Homestead Act of 1862 was intended to provide land to former slaves, but only four thousand out of four million blacks in the South submitted applications, in large part because blacks lacked the capital necessary to work the poor land that was on offer.[45] The Federal Housing Authority, established in 1934, practiced racial discrimination for many years in deciding who got cheap mortgages and who did not.[46] In the private sector as well, blacks suffered discrimination; less than 1 percent of all mortgages went to blacks between 1930 and 1960.[47] A 1991 study found that commercial banks rejected black mortgage applicants twice as often as they rejected white applicants.[48] The G.I. Bill of Rights that sent tens of thousands of veterans to college and provided hundreds of thousands with low-cost mortgages included numerous built-in barriers to black participation that only widened the black-white wealth gap.[49] The United States Department of Agriculture has acknowledged decades of discrimination against black farmers in its lending programs.[50]

Equality for African American women will never come in the United States until the state and federal governments address the legacy of unequal wealth accumulation begun in the slavery era. Today's unequal distribution of wealth is not the result of harder-working whites reaping their just rewards compared to good-for-nothing African Americans. It is the direct result of generations of whites exploiting black labor. Wealth gaps occur along both racial and gender lines, revealing themselves in terms of cultural capital such as networks developed through sports, camps, precollege education, contacts, friendship, and after-school activities; milestone life events, including gifts for college, weddings, and first-home purchase; and willed

44. Oliver and Shapiro, *Black Wealth, White Wealth*, 274.

45. Jay R. Mandle, "Continuity and Change: The Use of Black Labor after the Civil War," *Journal of Black Studies* 21 (1991), 420.

46. Oliver and Shapiro, *Black Wealth, White Wealth*, 17-18.

47. Meizhu Lui et al., *Color of Wealth*, 11.

48. Oliver and Shapiro, *Black Wealth, White Wealth*, 19.

49. Ira Katznelson, *When Affirmative Action Was White* (New York: Norton, 2006) 113-24.

50. Shaila K. Dewan, "Black Farmers' Refrain: Where's All Our Money?" *New York Times*, August 1, 2004.

assets after death.[51] This system of wealth differences began during the great suffering of the slave trade.

Though unpaid forced laborers, black women, through it all, maintained a faith in God's future justice, if not for themselves, then for their children and grandchildren. Enslaved women did not develop a systematic theology, still their experiences of justice and faith help us to create our own theology of justice.

Theology of Justice

Enslaved black women's historical experiences, connected with the effects of slavery that African American women still experience in today's socioeconomic system, suggest a way for us to create our own theology of justice.[52] This theology draws on the biblical emphasis on equality and justice in both the Old and New Testaments.

A Biblical Basis

African American women's cry for equality and justice in all of creation stresses the need for us to reread the Bible from the perspective of equality and justice. These women's experiences and faith inspire us to reinterpret the creation narrative in Genesis (of the Hebrew Scriptures) and understand what it tells us about the foundations of a healthy community. The principles of equality and justice described by these women can provide a lens through which to read scripture. For example, in Genesis, Yahweh takes dust and combines it with divine breath to give birth to humanity. And humanity is created to be in harmony with the rest of nature—birds, plants, fish, animals, air, water, wind, and earth. In Gen 1:26, a first command of the divinity is for humanity to be responsible stewards over all of the created order. Yahweh leases responsibility to all people to tend to the gardens of the Creator.

Symbolically, the sin of Adam and Eve lies in their turning away from the divine intention for humans to live in harmony with each other and with nature and adopting instead a focus on selfish individual pursuits. Enslaved

---

51. Oliver and Shapiro, *Black Wealth, White Wealth*, 154–59.

52. For extended treatment of enslaved women's theology, see Joan M. Martin, *More Than Chains and Toil: A Christian Work Ethic of Enslaved Women* (Louisville: Westminster John Knox, 2000); Dwight N. Hopkins and George C. L. Cummings, eds., *Cut Loose Your Stammering Tongue: Black Theology in the Slave Narrative*, 2nd ed. (Louisville: Westminster John Knox, 2003); and Hopkins, *Down, Up, and Over*.

black women longed for equal stewardship over all things and creatures on the earth. They believed that God would provide the opportunity for them to have wealth to enjoy family and experience the joy of living. Though injured by slavery, black women used a justice faith to repair damage done to them and their families. Sojourner Truth speaks to such a theological point in the following debate with a white slave mistress: "I tell you. I stretched up and felt as tall as the world. 'Missus,' says I, 'I'll have my son back again!' She laughed. 'You will, you nigger? How you goin' to do it? You ha'nt got no money.' 'No Missus but God has enough, or what's better! And I'll have my child again.'"[53]

Indeed, through the kindness of various people, including a group of Quakers in a neighboring town, Truth was introduced to and given money to pay for a sympathetic lawyer who found and returned her son. Truth understood this as fulfillment of her prayers to God, whose egalitarian goodness "shields the innocent, and causes them to triumph over their enemies."[54] Thus, God allowed Truth to share in divinely given wealth and obtain her son once again. The oppressor class assumes that wealth creation is their private privilege. They believe in Jesus but with a theology that separates his heavenly rule from the troubles and pain of the earthly world. But this theology contradicts the original creation story in which Yahweh leases responsibility to humankind as stewards, not as exploiters of black women's flesh. A theology of justice based on faith in universal access to the fruits of the world brought justice for Truth and can do so for contemporary African American women as well.

According to this reading of Genesis, all private goals of individual desire rather than communal good come from the original sin of the parents of all humankind. The primary theological point is that we are not working toward the God-given balance and harmony of equal sharing in divine creation. Consequently, restoring just relations requires sharing the aboundance of Yahweh's created order equally among all people.

Similarly, the experiences and faith of enslaved black women help us to read the Hebrew Scriptures as a liberation document offering justice to those at the bottom of society, those who have been wronged by the elite's hoarding of the world's resources. The ancient Israelite people had been held in slavery under one of the most powerful rulers at that time. The Egyptian pharaoh commanded a great army, much land, and enormous wealth. Yet Yahweh delivered these enchained workers and gave them

---

53. Quoted in Martin, *More Than Chains*, 82. See also Olive Gilbert, *Narrative of Sojourner Truth* (New York: Penguin, 1998), 30.

54. Gilbert, *Narrative of Sojourner Truth*, 20.

their share of the created order, symbolized by Canaan, the land flowing with milk and honey. For enslaved African American women hearing this story, the message is that Yahweh not only fights one's battles and achieves one's emancipation, the divinity also provides the provision of land, food, and other resources for the earth's poor to share in. Like Genesis, the sacred text helps us see a way to restore hope by working toward a world of equality and justice.

The Christian Scriptures

The Christian Scriptures also offer a religious basis of a theology of justice in which the bottom level of society wins the struggle to participate equally in God's creation. Martha Griffith Browne, writing in her autobiography after slavery was abolished, points to the inevitable judgment that plantation owners will face for their unjust treatment of others in God's creation. She uses the message of Jesus Christ as a lens for developing this idea. Mrs. Griffith Browne draws on the "sheep and goat" story in Matt 25, in which Jesus is the ultimate judge and provides the only criterion for entering heaven: Does one help the poor and oppressed? Slavery exploited and robbed one group within society, and its perpetrators will one-day face "the divine rule." The exploiters "will stand with a fearful accountability before the Supreme Judge. Then will there be loud cries and lamentations, and a wish for the mountains to hide [the slave masters] from the eye of Judicial Majesty."[55] The poor ultimately experience a new material reality where they participate equally in all that God has created. In her specific reference to Matthew 25, Mrs. Griffith Browne points to the only place in the Christian Bible where Jesus gives direct, unambiguous instructions on how Christians are to enter heaven. Here heaven is a new social arrangement; it is shared wealth and social harmony. Mrs. Griffith Browne read the Bible and concluded that justice is restored to those who aid the oppressed.

The fact that Matthew concludes its story with the entrance into a new society based on the sharing of the divine gifts is not surprising. Jesus ends where he began in the Christian Scriptures. The slave community was well aware of the book of Luke chapter 4, where Jesus gives his first public sermon or speech. A divinity incarnated on earth reveals the sole purpose of the divine among humankind—to preach good news to the poor, to announce release for all captives, to give sight to the blind, to set at liberty those who are oppressed, and to realize Jubilee—the year of universal emancipation.

55. Martha Griffith Browne, *Autobiography of a Female Slave* (1857; reprint, New York: Negro Universities Press, 1969), 21–22.

Jesus's sole intent through his birth stories and life on earth was to break the chains preventing the dispossessed from becoming full human beings equal to all others. And Jesus, as Mrs. Griffith Browne read Matt 25, would make a way out of no way to bring this about.

Conclusion

The historical experiences, faith, and biblical interpretations of enslaved black women examined in this chapter can assist us on the path to recognizing the need for and creating a theology of justice. One key to this search for a theology of justice is the following: We must begin to see a theology of justice as a way to assign collective accountability for slavery and its consequences. Today's black/white and black woman's/white woman's wealth gaps do not come primarily from whites' hard work and blacks' laziness. The gap comes from inherited economic, political, and social advantages and inherited economic, political, and social disadvantages.

As Sheila Briggs states: "Whites have inherited advantages simply through their membership in a trans-historical community that has accumulated the material resources that were produced in slavery and a later racially discriminatory society. Since individual benefit depends on collective identity, then moral responsibility for the injustice of wealth distribution cannot be restricted to a purely personal and individual level, but must be assigned to the trans-historical social group that collectively enjoyed the benefits."[56]

In sum, while whites have continued to benefit from wealth held by whites, blacks continue to suffer the economic, political, and social costs of their lack of wealth, which is a direct result of the slavery era. One group has consistently benefited from black labor, and another has consistently suffered. The historical facts and the lives and beliefs of enslaved black women together encourage us to position collective responsibility at the center of a theology of just reparations. Healing would benefit the children of both the slave owner and the enslaved. Restorative justice with forgiveness and reconciliation presents one path toward a healthy America.

---

56. From e-mail correspondence with Sheila Briggs on April 2, 2008.

9

Black Women's Spirituality of Funk

> I have to trust the uncontrolled, wild parts of myself, it's really dangerous ... What was valued was [Nel and Sula's] friendship ... it was spiritual, of first order priority; the "other I." —Toni Morrison[1]

From slavery until today, African American women have contributed their unique spirituality to black survival and liberation. In the face of (white and black) male and (white) female discriminations, African American women have simply claimed their right to be God's children on earth. Often they acted out their leadership roles in traditional church structures. In other situations, they created new models of religious practice however and whenever they felt called to say and do God's word of freedom. Black women expressed emancipating spiritual power on divine and not "man's" agenda.

Today African American women religious scholars name their survival and liberation God-experiences as "womanist theology." Womanist theologians acknowledge a belief connection to all humanity, whether male or female, black or white. Yet there is a difference. And it is this disturbing and freeing uniqueness that black women celebrate. It is disturbing because, for too long, others have attempted to stifle God's winds of spiritual life in African American women. It is freeing because no human denials can forever keep hidden the persistent presence of a spirit-filled black woman.

In fact Jacquelyn Grant raised this challenge in the first womanist article in the contemporary period. She accused black theology of maintaining the invisibility of African American women. How could a (male)

---

1. Quoted in Sandi Russell, "'It's OK to Say OK,'" in *Critical Essays on Toni Morrison*, ed. Nellie Y. McKay (Boston: Hall, 1988), 45 and 46.

black theology lift the banner of liberation when black women suffer from the pains of gender discrimination?[2] Noting their absence, womanists have mapped out their permanent presence in all theology. In the words of womanist Katie G. Cannon: "Black women live out a moral wisdom in their real-lived context that does not appeal to the fixed rules of absolute principles of the white-oriented, male-structured society. Black women's analysis and appraisal of what is right or wrong and good or bad develop out of the various coping mechanisms related to the conditions of their own cultural circumstances."[3] Womanists bring fresh air to the discussion. They are less inhibited by the constraints of "orthodox" (read: standard Euro-American and male) doctrines. Such freshness breathes a newness more akin to what God would have us do to free black people from heinous external structures and debilitating internal self-destruction.

For instance, Delores S. Williams has looked into literary fiction (in her "Black Women's Literature and the Task of Feminist Theology") and named "a language of the spirit" (in her "Womanist Theology: Black Women's Voices"). And it is this spirit talking that has taken the women beyond traditional boundaries, out to the margins, into the mainstream, wherever they want to go in the church, society, the Bible, and educational institutions for discovering (and declaring) their own voices.[4]

Clearly a constructive black liberation theology needs African American women's spirituality as a resource. And the "uncontrolled" and "dangerous" dimensions of Toni Morrison's fictional female communities offer such a fertile starting point for constructive work. The theological imagination in Morrison's characters helps us to understand poor black women's spirituality as a cornerstone of theological development.

In Morrison's novels, poor black women's spirituality is a revelation of God's spirit of liberation incarnated in their traditions. Such a spirit incarnates in particular women while, simultaneously, transcending the limitations of a single individual. In fact, the power of poor black women's traditions lies in their ability to deliver and sustain each succeeding generation, thus their example of immortality. Spirituality lives in concrete people, which alerts us to the fact that we only know the work of the spirit by finding

---

2. Jacquelyn Grant, "Black Theology and Black Women," in *Black Theology: A Documentary History, 1966-1979*, eds. Gayraud S. Wilmore and James H. Cone (Maryknoll, NY: Orbis, 1979), 418-33.

3. "Moral Wisdom in the Black Women's Literary Tradition," *The Annual of the Society of Christian Ethics*, ed. Larry Rasmussen (1984) 175.

4. Williams's two articles, respectively, appear in *Immaculate and Powerful: The Female in Sacred Image and Social Reality*, ed. C. W. Atkinson et al. (Boston: Beacon, 1985), 88-109; and *Christianity and Crisis* (March 2, 1987) 66-70.

it as it works in specific human traditions. Real incarnation shows us material reality. Yet, though the spirit lives in identifiable groups of women, it goes beyond them. Transcendence means beyond the material. God, therefore, is a spiritual presence who is greater than (i.e., transcends) the Christian and non-Christian representations in any one person or community found in Toni Morrison's stories.

To discover a deeper understanding of poor black women's spirituality and its challenges and comprehensive contributions to black theology, then, this chapter will first examine Morrison's own use of the terms "the Thing" and "the Funk" in their connection to African American women's spiritual practices and, second, will develop an extended treatment of actual traditions that are at the heart of that same spirituality.

The poor black women in these stories act out their faith in God's spirit of liberation through their traditions. God's spirit of liberation and poor black women's faith in this spirit appear in traditions energizing the entire lives of these women. These women do not do theology with proclamations of systematic dogma. Poor African American women do not have the privilege to write. However, it is the theologian's task (1) to make clear the spiritual movement of God's freedom in the midst of these women's practical activity and (2) to systematize their practical activity of faith in God's spirit of justice. Thus a spirituality coming out of black women's faith experiences pushes black theology to work with God's comprehensive liberation.

The Thing and the Funk

The Thing is a demonic, sterile, and life-denying spirituality that oppresses poor black women. Consequently, one cannot understand their spirituality without noting the context in which these women find themselves. In contrast to the Thing, the Funk includes women's spirit of liberation (found in traditions) used by poor black women in order to survive and free themselves from the evil grip of the Thing.

The Thing

In *The Bluest Eye*, Claudia (a very poor African American girl who narrates Morrison's first novel) pinpoints the all-encompassing presence of the Thing when she comments: "The Thing to fear was the Thing that made her beautiful, and not us."[5] The "her" refers to a new girl in school, a half white

---

5. See *Bluest Eye* (New York: Washington Square, 1970), 62.

"high-yellow dream child" with "sloe green eyes."[6] The "us" refers to poor black females such as Claudia. The Thing symbolizes the totality of black women's oppression. Essentially, it means a sinister spirituality that interweaves throughout all forms of oppression faced by these women. It is both a political attack, in the sense that it blocks black women's power to control their own space that they occupy on earth; and it is a cultural attack, in the sense that it negatively defines the identity of African American women. In a word, the Thing represents an attempt to negate God's spirit of liberation expressed through poor black women. Thus a war unfolds between suffering brought about by the demonic, on the one hand, and grace freely given by God's spirit, on the other.

More specifically, Claudia fleshes out the face of the Thing's spirit in the following observation: "Everybody in the world was in a position to give [poor black women] orders. White women said, 'Do this.' White children said, 'Give me that.' White men said, 'Come here.' Black men said, 'Lay down.' They had carried a world on their heads."[7]

Here in Toni Morrison's writings, poor black women face triple expressions of the spirit of the Thing. These women share the unique spiritual pain of three sectors of North American society—the subordinate status of women (victims of white and black male dominance), the objects of racism (white male and female supremacy), and the plight of the poor (economic exploitation). The convergence of these three realities exists only for poor African American women. They carry "a world on their heads." As women, they are victimized by the desires of both white and black males ("Come here" and "Lay down"). As African Americans, they experience racism from both white men and white women ("Come here" and "Do this"). And as mere labor commodities, they are subjected to the foreman-like commands represented by little white children ("Give me that"). In sum the politics and culture of the Thing reveal themselves in the totality of poor black women's lives through a complicated web of gender, race and poverty, which strangles the spirit of these women.

Gender

As women, the characters in Toni Morrison's novels confront the spirituality of the Thing defining both their cultural identity (as objects satisfying the sexual appetite of men) and their political identity (as objects lacking self-determination and independence from men's power and control). For

6. Ibid., 52 and 53.
7. Ibid., 109 and 110.

example, two white males on the Sweet Home plantation in *Beloved* rape the slave woman Sethe.[8] They do not violate in the classic understanding of rape; there is no forced vaginal penetration. However, their violation of Sethe points to an even more violent rape of her own definition of her female self. What these spiritually sick, white fictional characters do instead is to knock her to the ground in a barn and suck her milk from her breasts. Sethe oozed with milk because she was full of drink for her baby daughter. Though the two rapists see Sethe as merely a cow, without a spirit, in fact, the taking of her milk means the very theft of that which represents one of the defining characteristics of her spiritual motherness—part of the essence, which defines her culturally as a woman. So these white men forcefully take the life-essence material and spiritual food for her child.

Similarly, Ella, another poor black woman in *Beloved*, accounts for the degree of white male, slave owner sexual pathology by "the lowest yet." Ella's "puberty was spent in a house were she was shared by father and son, whom she called 'the lowest.'" Ella did not have the power to name her spiritual identity as a woman during her teenage and young adult life. On the contrary, she grew up as a plaything to gratify the sick sexual taste of a white father-son tag team. Because her womanist spirit suffered such a grave violation in so many unspeakable acts and for so many years, Ella measured all attacks on women through her own historical confrontation with the Thing. "A killing, a kidnap, a rape . . . Nothing compared to the 'lowest yet.'"[9]

The poor black women of Morrison's stories also experience lack of gender self-definition in several of their relationships with black men. Milkman, the protagonist in *Song of Solomon*, tires of sexually conquering his cousin Hagar because he no longer feels that she is a challenge to his warped, male sexual ego. And furthermore, given the ratio of black men to women in the novel, he believes he can pick and choose his sexual objects from black or white females. Thinking about the years of his affair with Hagar, Milkman surmises: "Now, after more than a dozen years, he was getting tired of her. Her eccentricities were no longer provocative and the stupefying ease with which he had gotten and stayed between her legs had changed from the great good fortune he'd considered it, to annoyance at her refusal to make him hustle for it." Milkman no longer defines Hagar as a woman, but "the third beer . . . The third, the one you drink because . . . what difference does it make?"[10] He describes part of her womanist nature as a beer—a thing without a "difference," without a spirit.

---

8. Toni Morrison, *Beloved: A Novel* (New York: Knopf, 1987), 15–17.
9. Ibid., 256.
10. Toni Morrison, *Song of Solomon* (New York: Knopf, 1977), 91.

Likewise in *The Bluest Eye*, Pauline Breedlove, a poor black woman with a disabled foot, suffers from her husband's distorted definition of their marriage. At the beginning of their relationship, both saw their sexuality as an equal sharing of their mutual spiritual selves. For her, it used to "be rainbow all inside." Later her husband, Cholly, treats her as a mere receptor of his physical release. Analyzing the latter part of their marriage, Pauline says: "But it ain't like that anymore. Most times he's thrashing away inside me before I'm woke, and through when I am."[11]

But some black males' inclination to define black women as pleasure receptors in Morrison's novels does not begin with the later institution of marriage. For some, this naming starts with little black girls. For instance, Nel and Sula, the two main characters in *Sula*, always experience catcalls and receive new names whenever these two children walk past the Time and a Half Pool Hall in order to get to an ice cream store. Old and young black men lustfully watch them. "Nel and Sula walked through this valley of eyes chilled by the wind and heated by the embarrassment of appraising stares . . . Pig meat. The words were in all [the men's] minds."[12]

However, the spirit of the Thing does not only deny African American women's spirituality by culturally defining women's sexuality in a patriarchal way. It also takes away women's political right to self-determination. The Thing prevents the free spirit of womanist spirituality and thus determines, controls, and maps out what is woman's space and place. Again in *Sula* we find Nel and Sula in conversation, but this time they are discussing whether or not a woman has the power to control her own life independently. In a moment of submission to the power of the Thing, Nel tells Sula: "You can't have it all, Sula . . . You can't do it all. You a woman and a colored woman at that. You can't act like a man. You can't be walking around all independent-like, doing whatever you like, taking what you want, leaving what you don't."[13]

Here Nel cannot imagine a womanist spirituality that lets women make decisions about their own lives independently of men. Note how Nel does not tell Sula to decide and claim her own space by herself and then raise her own views to a man. No. Nel warns Sula to make all decisions as an absolute appendage to a man, furthermore implying that women's alternatives and ideas about place are subordinate to men's.

---

11. Morrison, *Bluest Eye*, 104.
12. Toni Morrison, *Sula* (New York: Knopf, 1973), 50.
13. Ibid., 142.

Race

The Thing's demonic spirituality expresses itself by denying black women the freedom to control the spiritual definition of their own gender. In this sense womanist spirituality connects with white women who suffer from patriarchy. We see this in an encounter between Sethe and Amy, a poor white woman in *Beloved*. Sethe has escaped from slavery but lives on the verge of death. While Sethe thinks about her mortality out in the woods, Amy comes along and nurses Sethe back to life and sends Sethe to the next stop on her freedom journey. Amy tells Sethe how she (Amy) was an indentured servant fleeing from whippings and the cruelty of the male patriarchy. Both women have been objects of male dominance; in this regard, they are spiritual mates.

Yet not only does the Thing attack black women's reality in the area of gender; it also separates black women's spirituality from that of white women because of racial discrimination.[14] Although Amy heals Sethe's feet and tends to the bruises on her back, thus showing a common gender solidarity, Amy still calls Sethe a "nigger." Likewise, Sethe still has to call Amy "ma'am."[15] Thus, the Thing is more wicked for poor black women. Therefore, even within black-white sister spirituality, black women suffer more because white culture rules as the standard.

The same white-skinned privileges separate black and white female relations in *Tar Baby*. Margaret Street prides herself for her classic white liberal attitude toward her black cook, Ondine. Historically, Margaret used to spend hours talking with Ondine and even working in the kitchen with her. But when Ondine begins to publicly expose Margaret because Margaret tortured her own son, Margaret puts Ondine in her place by shouting at Ondine: "Shut up! You nigger! You nigger bitch!"[16] Here Margaret practices white women's option to exercise their white cultural privileges over poor African American women. Margaret unleashes her white power to define Ondine's black identity as a female dog.

Indeed, the Thing begins to work against a positive womanist racial spirituality at a very young age. In *Sula*, the little black girl Nel has to

---

14. This is what Alice Walker means when she defines womanist in *In Search of Our Mothers' Gardens* (New York: Harcourt Brace Jovanovich, 1983), xii. "Womanist is to feminist as purple to lavender," writes Walker. Specifically, black and white women both endure male chauvinism and thus overlap in a common spirituality, like purple and lavender. But just as purple is not quite lavender, so too African American women's spirituality differs form white feminism due to white women's potential participation in white male supremacy against black women.

15. *Beloved*, 31ff and 78–85.

16. *Tar Baby* (New York: New American Library, 1981), 208.

continually hear commands from her own mother (Mrs. Wright), who tells her to pull her nose with a clothespin and thus make her black nose white.

> When Mrs. Wright reminded Nel to pull her nose, she would do it enthusiastically but without the least hope in the world.
>
> "While you sittin' there, honey, go 'head and pull your nose."
>
> "It hurts, Mamma."
>
> "Don't you want a nice nose when you grow up?"[17]

A nice pair of nostrils is a white woman's nose because the African cultural features of poor black women must be destroyed with a clothespin, even if "It hurts, Mamma."

But the depth of the Thing's white supremacy in the lives of poor black women reveals itself most pointedly in *The Bluest Eye*. "It had begun with Christmas and the gift of dolls. The big, the special, the loving gift was always a big, blue-eyed Baby Doll," narrates little black girl Claudia.[18] For her, these valuable Christmas gifts symbolized the ongoing attempt by society to crush the beauty of her black culture. Society told her that the essence of beauty was a blond, blue-eyed Shirley Temple doll with pale skin and rosy cheeks. "I knew," continues Claudia, "that the doll represented what they thought was my fondest wish." Consequently, from the Thing's demonic perspective, to love Shirley Temple meant loving the essence of womanist spirituality. Summing up the process that denied her own African American cultural identity, Claudia concludes: "Adults, older girls, shops, magazines, newspapers, window signs—all the world had agreed that a blue-eyed, yellow-haired, pink-skinned doll was what every girl child treasured. 'Here,' they said, 'this is beautiful, and if you are on this day "worthy" you may have it.'"[19]

For black women, to be "worthy" of the gift of whiteness can drive you insane. In fact, Pecola, one of Claudia's black playmates, does exactly that. After believing that she has finally received the gift of blue eyes, Pecola suffers a mental derailment and goes insane. She "stepped over into madness" and was forever seen "searching the garbage" heaps while both of her arms twitched like chicken wings.[20] The Thing succeeded with Pecola, a beautiful, poor little black girl. It broke her own self-love for her cultural identity. It forced her into a psychological suicide in quest for a sickly female whiteness. And it disintegrated her into the realm of spiritual self-destruction.

17. Ibid., 55.
18. *Bluest Eye*, 19.
19. Ibid., 20.
20. Ibid., 159 and 160.

Though, as I stated earlier, gender oppression unites black and white women's spirituality (against men, white and black); racial discrimination (perpetrated by whites, male and female) links womanist spirituality with the survival of the entire African American community. When it comes to white supremacy, the Thing knows no gender difference for black people. For instance in *Beloved*, Stamp Paid, an old black man who helps slaves escape on the Underground Railroad, sums up the Thingness of white oppression. He reflects on the years of lynchings ("human blood cooked in a lynch fire" so much that the "stench stank"), genocide ("Whole towns wiped clean of Negroes"), whippings, schools burned, and property stolen. Stamp concludes with a question to the divine: "What are these people? You tell me, Jesus. What are they?"[21] Not who are they, questions Stamp, but what type of Thing were white folk anyway?

Poverty

Finally, the oppressive spirit of the Thing displays itself by putting black women into poverty. We have seen poor black women victimized politically and culturally by male-gender chauvinism, and culturally by white racial discrimination. The Thing also spreads its kingdom to include economic exploitation—poverty. In this way, black women lack the political right and power to determine the destiny of their own daily sustenance and livelihood.

The majority of Toni Morrison's main characters find themselves trapped in a web of forced economic inequality.[22] These are hardworking black mothers, grandmothers, sisters, daughters, and wives struggling to hold on to a job or fighting to make a way out of no way.

> They ran the houses of white people, and knew it. When white men beat their men, they cleaned up the blood and went home to receive abuse from the victim. They beat their children with one hand and stole for them with the other. The hands that felled trees also cut umbilical cords; the hands that wrung the necks of chickens and butchered hogs also nudged African violets into bloom; the arms that loaded sheaves, bales, and sacks rocked babies into sleep. They patted biscuits into flaky ovals of

---

21. *Beloved*, 180.

22. Even Jadine in *Tar Baby* originated from a poor working class background. And, though a recent member of the black middle income group, she still struggles with the spiritual roots of her African American ancestry and the anemic spiritual aspirations of the white petty bourgeoisie.

innocence—and shrouded the dead. They plowed all day and came home to nestle like plums under the limbs of their men.[23]

More specifically, Pauline Breedlove (*The Bluest Eye*) worked as a cook and laundry woman in the house of middle-income white people. A slave on the Sweet Home plantation, Baby Suggs (*Beloved*) worked in the Big House. Eva Peace (*Sula*) raised her children on three beets. Some people rumored that she later left town and cut off her own leg in order to collect insurance money for her children's survival. Pilate Dead (*Song of Solomon*) was a bootlegger. And Therese, the blind woman, held an occasional washerwoman position while her friend, Alma Estee, cleaned toilets at the airport (*Tar Baby*).

Furthermore, the poverty status of African American women in Morrison's novels also teaches us how the Thing's spirit caused class divisions among black women, thus emphasizing the unique assault on poor black women's spirituality. For instance, Geraldine, a bourgeois colored woman, taught her son, Junior, the class distinctions within the black community. "She had explained to him the difference between colored people and niggers. They were easily identifiable. Colored people were neat and quiet; niggers were dirty and loud."[24] One day Junior tricks Pecola, a poor little black girl, into his house. When his mother, Geraldine, eventually arrives home, she looks at Pecola. "Saw the dirty torn dress, the plaits sticking out on her head, hair matted where the plaits had come undone, the muddy shoes with the wad of gum peeping out from between the cheap soles, the soiled socks . . . She saw the safety pin holding the hem of the dress up." With hatred, revulsion, and a coldblooded spirituality, colored Geraldine stares at little black Pecola and says: "Get out . . . You nasty little black bitch. Get out of my house."[25]

But the class divide (the Thing's spirituality of poverty) is more than an individual demon in Morrison's narratives. It also reflects a systemic economic evil, which reduces poor African American women to mere labor commodities in human relations based on ruthless, uncaring profit. As a result, these women do not control their lives economically and politically.

Perhaps Valerian Street, a white entrepreneur in *Tar Baby*, represents this economic realty most clearly. Valerian inherits a capitalist corporation making candy. Not wanting to spend the rest of his life "working" too hard, he purchases an island in the Caribbean and retires there. One Christmas, he immediately fires two poor Caribbean servants because they merely take

23. *Bluest Eye*, 109–10.
24. Ibid., 71.
25. Ibid., 75.

some apples to eat. Son, a mysterious black visitor at Valerian's island home, describes the exploitative spiritual traditions of Valerian and the economic system they represent:

> [Valerian] had been able to dismiss with a flutter of the fingers the people whose sugar and cocoa had allowed him to grow old in regal comfort; although he had taken the sugar and cocoa and paid for it as though it had no value, as though the cutting of cane and picking of beans was child's play and had no value; but he turned it into candy, the invention of which really was child's play, and sold it to other children and made a fortune.

Linking Valerian and his economic system to the demonic, Son tells how Valerian paid poor people "according to some scale of value that would outrage Satan himself." But these harmful spiritual traditions did not surprise the poor because the rich "loved property," so much that "they had killed it soiled it defecated on it."[26]

Accordingly, the Thing's spirit actively lives in the gender, racial, and poverty persecution and repression of poor African American women. Essentially, the spirit of the Thing comes from a larger theological idea held by white males with privileges in the novels. Commenting on Sethe (who has just attempted to "free" her children by killing them and thus prevent a return to slavery on the Sweet Home plantation), Schoolteacher (a white overseer on the same plantation) arrogantly remarks: "see what happened when you overbeat creatures God had given you the responsibility of."[27] Consequently, these white men have faith in a theology in which God's spirit has anointed them to be responsible over poor black women. This is the essence of the Thing.

The Funk

Given the reality of the Thing, who will speak for these poor African American women? Who will defend their unique cultural identities and the right to determine their own political space on this earth? Fundamentally for a Christian the question is whether or not God has forgotten the cries and predicament of these "little ones" and has left them to the devilish spirit of the Thing. Quite the contrary, God's grace has given these women the liberating spirituality of the Funk.

---

26. *Tar Baby*, 203.
27. *Beloved*, 150.

Below, under the section "Traditions," we will develop a detailed and systematic treatment of womanist spirituality (or the Funk) as it is revealed specifically in the traditions of poor black women. However, in general terms, womanist spirituality can be defined as the Funk—including the resources for survival and freedom given by the divine spirit living in the total lives of the women found in Toni Morrison's novels. The Funk is a free spirit constantly warding off the Thing's oppressive attacks.

In *The Bluest Eye*, Morrison highlights the intentional designs of the Thing when it grooms and prepares a section of African American women to defeat the Funk. Black women susceptible to the Thing's power, Morrison writes, "go to land-grant colleges, normal schools, and learn how to do the white man's work with refinement: home economics to prepare his food; teacher education to instruct black children in obedience; music to soothe the weary master and entertain his blunted soul . . . In short, how to get rid of the funkiness of the wide range of human emotions." The Thing does not want black women to have a humanity or human spirit ("the wide range of human emotions"). Over against the God-given spirituality of these women (that is, the funkiness of their created nature and the funkiness of their passion for a total liberated existence), the Thing seeks to convert these women into a life of dead spirituality, where poor black women no longer have their own identities and power to control their own lives. Referencing the struggle between the Thing and the Funk, Morrison resumes: "Wherever it erupts, this Funk, they wipe it away." The battle between the authority of the Funk (womanist spirituality empowered by the presence of God's spirit of liberation) and the authority of the Thing (the political and cultural spiritual death of gender discrimination, racial oppression, and poverty exploitation) continues "all the way to the grave."[28]

Oftentimes those controlled by the Thing call the Funk "wild blood." In *Sula*, Helene Sabat's mother was a Creole sex worker in New Orleans. Both Helene and her grandmother detested the profession of Helene's mother. Overreacting to the mother's immoral activities, the grandmother removes Helene from her mother and also crushes any sense of womanist spirituality in Helene. "The grandmother took Helene away from the soft lights and flowered carpets of the Sundown [prostitution] House and raised her under the dolesome eyes of a multicolored Virgin Mary, counseling her to be constantly on guard for any sign of her mother's wild blood."[29] Here we discover how the deadly spirit of the Thing can disguise itself under the mantle of authentic Christianity in order to control the liberating spirit of

28. *Bluest Eye*, 68.
29. *Sula*, 17.

the Funk by characterizing it as wild blood. Helene grew up worshiping a sorrowful and melancholy Virgin Mary. All her life she believed in a white gloomy, grief-filled Christianity that taught African American women not to free themselves but, rather, to maintain the status quo of gender, racial, and poverty enslavement.

Yet the Funk persists. It empowers poor black women to confront face-to-face powerful representatives of the Thing. After sixteen years of slaving for a white male of privilege (a Mr. Sawyer), Sethe (*Beloved*) finally reacts "wildly" to her boss. She boldly states, "Don't talk to me, Mr. Sawyer. Don't say nothing to me this morning." Responding to Sethe's declaration of womanist independence as if she has gone completely insane, Sawyer replies: "What? What? What? You talking back to me?" Sethe tenaciously holds her ground and shouts, "I'm telling you don't say nothing to me."[30] It appears as if God's spirit of liberation had finally surrounded Sethe and moved her to act freely. The fact that she took the risk to defend herself against Sawyer, her employer, was no small matter. Because her income from this job helped to feed and keep her children alive, her move toward freedom of the Funk could have brought literal starvation and death to her family.

The Funk not only allows poor African American women to stand up against a wicked gender-racial-poverty spirituality; it also gives them confidence to move beyond the boundaries defined by the Thing. Gripped by womanist spirituality, Sula Peace, in *Sula*, one day decides to travel and educate herself. Without announcement, she departs from her small hometown and in the next ten years goes to college and travels to Nashville, Detroit, New Orleans, New York, Philadelphia, Macon, and San Diego. In the 1920s, it would have been extremely difficult for a black person, a poor person, or a woman to move about independently across the U.S. without the authority of a white person, a rich person, or a male of privilege. Yet Sula's Funk empowers her to travel beyond the prohibited boundaries of gender, racial, and poverty restrictions. Her funky free passion for a complete life allows her to define herself culturally as a free black woman. And, consequently, she takes the risk to define politically what to do in life and where to walk on earth. Her self-definition and self-direction beyond the status-quo boundaries represent the freeing spirit of the Funk.

We have seen how the Funk is womanist spirituality—God's spirit of liberation living and incarnated in poor black women's total reality. This spirit of freedom anoints them to challenge the rule of the Thing. In opposition, the demonic spirit of the Thing (expressed through gender, racial, and poverty inequalities) doggedly hounds poor black women.

30. *Beloved*, 62.

Culturally the Thing produces a sterile spirituality and prevents the naming of women's self; no longer are women themselves and connected to themselves. Once the Thing grips them culturally (that is, it defines their selves as something else), they also become a political supporter of their own three-pronged oppression.

On the other hand the Funk undermines the Thing culturally and politically. God's spirit of liberation gives women the power to know themselves and to be connected to themselves culturally. The ability to know who they are and thus define themselves aids these women in the transformation of the conditions in which they find themselves politically. And the ability to determine and change the space and conditions around them, in turn, provides these women more freedom to further define themselves. In brief, freedom to be themselves (a cultural act of spiritual liberation) stands in a vibrant relationship with freedom to determine their space (a political act of spiritual liberation). The politics and culture of womanist spirituality work together.

Now, having established the context of and the need for poor African American women's spirituality in opposition to the Thing and having explored womanist spirituality in general terms with an explanation of the Funk, we can move to a systematic examination of the heart of womanist spirituality—God's spirit of liberation incarnated in poor black women's traditions of embodiment.

Traditions of Embodiment

Traditions of embodiment include four categories—tradition of embodiment in poor black women themselves, in their immediate community, in their broader community, and in nature. Traditions are theological and spiritual experiences of wisdom shared with and passed on from women to women and in the interest of all people. Put differently, sacred knowledge of survival, struggle, and freedom accumulates from and stretches to women to women, thus gathering an immortal body of traditions that surpass and enlarge the strength of each individual woman.

Embodiment in Herself

Within themselves Toni Morrison's black female characters represent the tradition of conjurer. Conjurer women are usually associated with spiritual activities, which do not equal Christian practices. Yet a timeless spiritual power of liberation reflects itself in the religious functioning of these very same women. Thus the traditional embodiment of conjurer, lived out by poor black women, challenges black theology to recognize and create a space for a non-Christian reality of God's freeing representations. Will black theology acknowledge conjurers as legitimate sources for the actual doing of theology?

Restated, the Christian church is the largest organized form of religion within the black community. And for Christians who develop black theology, Jesus the Christ (i.e., the anointed one) remains the decisive revelation for their liberation faith experience with God. However, at the same time, a liberating African American theology must see the possibility of conjurers (i.e., an important part of womanist spirituality) complementing the Christ and increasing the liberation and formation of the new humanity. God's love for the poor produced the Messiah; yet the power of God's love for freedom did not and has not stopped in those places where the name of Jesus remains unknown. In those latter places, God has provided an anointing and revelation of a just spirit through other instruments of divine purpose.

In general terms, the conjurer women in Morrison's stories act as natural healers and saviors.[31] And while drawing on God's spirit in nature and the collective might of other poor black women, they work alongside Christians. Examining several women in Morrison's novels will show the conjurer as a tradition of embodiment within black women themselves.

In *Song of Solomon*, Pilate learns the wisdom and practices of conjuring from a black female migrant worker in New York who initiates and trains Pilate in the intricacies of root work, human relations to nature, and the untapped power within the human self. Referencing why she remained with a band of migrant bean pickers in New York, Pilate refers to her conjuring apprenticeship as the primary reason. "The main reason I stayed on," she relates, "was a woman there I took to. A root worker. She taught me a lot." Pilate decides to learn a freeing spiritual craft in order to further define her female self-identity and thereby accomplish an act of cultural practice.

The meeting between this experienced female conjurer and Pilate shows, in one sense, the ability of veterans in the field to consciously train and make other poor black women have the expertise of dealing in spirits. However, the beginner must also have a special and natural relation to spiritual matters. The power and gift of divine spirituality has to set her aside, in other words. And like Christian prophetesses and priestesses, conjurer women work on behalf of the people, yet they are not quite similar to those

31. In addition to characters mentioned in the text, other examples of healing-saving conjurer women are Ella, "a practical woman who believed there was a root either to chew or avoid for every ailment" (*Beloved*, 256); and Circe, "healer and deliverer," who saves the life of Pilate and Macon Dead the elder (*Song of Solomon*, 248).

for whom they struggle to bring about peace and justice. Accordingly, Pilate "was a natural healer, and among quarreling drunks and fighting women she could hold her own, and sometimes mediated a peace that lasted a good bit longer than it should have because it was administered by someone not like them." Thus a natural conjurer lives to serve the community. Above we see Pilate placing herself in the conflicts of people around her and, due to her special anointing, providing a healing peace to the lowly in society. Her power to resolve contradictions among poor folk comes from her spiritual anointing found in her special role—that is, the "someone not like them" points to her ability to have a justice interest in the affairs of her people.

Indeed, particularly relating to saving life, conjurers in Toni Morrison's stories seem to work for goodness wherever there exist evil spirits who would bring death. For instance, when Macon Dead the elder attempts to violently and viciously cause his own wife to have an abortion, the wife seeks out Pilate to save herself and the life of the fetus. For the strength of the mother and the child developing in her womb, Pilate prescribes crunchy foods (such as cornstarch, cracked ice, and nuts). For Macon Dead the elder, Pilate places on his chair a small "doll with a small painted chicken bone stuck between its legs and a round red circle painted on its belly". As a result, the expectant mother grew stronger and gave birth to a healthy baby boy who, as Macon Dead the younger, carried on the family tree and, thus, the life of the Dead family.[32] The right to determine life through conjuring spirituality highlights Pilate's fierce passion to promote the health of victimized black folk and their right to decide space around them—an act of politics.

Periodically the community in which the conjurer woman functions feels threatened due to its incorrect understanding of God's revelation of God's spirit through different human practices. This particularly applies to insecure Christians who pit God's spirit of liberation revealed in Jesus Christ over against the same spirit of liberation discovered in others. Even when the conjurer woman brings food and life within community (similar to the nourishing of Jesus), she risks potential isolation from her own benefactors. Baby Suggs experiences the effects of this blind, narrow type of Christianity when she increases meals for the poor black community she loves and is a part of. "[For Baby Suggs] to take two buckets of blackberries and make ten, maybe twelve, pies; to have turkey enough for the whole town pretty near, new peas in September, fresh cream but no cow, ice and sugar,

---

32. See *Song of Solomon*, 142, 150, and 132, for references to Pilate's abilities and feats. Furthermore, other indications of Pilate's love of community and unique spiritual gifts are found in the following description on 94: "never bothered anybody, was helpful to everybody, but who also was believed to have the power to step out of her skin, set a bush afire from fifty yards, and turn a man into a ripe rutabaga."

batter bread, bread pudding, raised bread, shortbread—it made them [her neighbors] mad. Loaves and fishes were His powers—they did not belong to an ex-slave."[33] The conjurer risks such potential attacks and possible misinterpreted acts of healing and saving in community because she has received an unsought-after ordaining by the spirit of God's word. At one point, Baby Suggs struggles against her calling due to the death and injury caused by white slave owners and a slave catcher coming on her property. But her colleague, Stamp Paid, reminds her: "Listen here, girl . . . you can't quit the Word. It's given to you to speak."[34]

Finally, conjurers (e.g., a tradition of embodiment within poor black women themselves) in womanist spirituality complement the spiritual power of Jesus Christ. For instance, Baby Suggs is both a Christian ("I did get to church every Sunday some kind of way," she says) and a nonconventional "unchurched preacher" whose compassionate heart increases with God's spirit in nature (e.g., she preaches at the Clearing, her sanctuary deep in the woods). In a similar way, when black women come to exorcise the she-devil spirit called Beloved from the black community, "Some brought what they could and what they believed would work. Stuffed in apron pockets, strung around their necks, lying in the space between their breasts. Others brought Christian faith—as shield and sword. Most brought a little of both."[35]

Furthermore, the complementary nature of Christian spirit and conjurer spirit in the act of saving and healing appears in *The Bluest Eye*. In one part of the story, an Aunt Jimmy borders on death. To halt the slow decline of their friend, her neighbors read her the Bible with no success. Finally, they call on a male Christian preacher and a female healer-savior named M'Dear, who approach Aunt Jimmy's bedside together. M'Dear lived quietly in a shack near the woods; and "any illness that could not be handled by ordinary means—known cures, intuition, or endurance—the word was always, 'Fetch M'Dear.'"[36] The conjurer woman, in this instance, provides the cure, which temporarily saves Aunt Jimmy's life. Though the Christian preacher remains outwardly silent, in fact, the combined spiritual strength of both Christian and conjurer helps the ailing Aunt Jimmy.

Embodying within themselves the tradition of conjurer, poor black women, thus, offer a valuable and untapped resource for creating a

33. *Beloved*, 137.

34. Ibid., 177.

35. See *Beloved*, 146 and 87, for both quoted descriptions of Baby Suggs's Christian and unorthodox faith. And view 257 for a depiction of the Christian and non-Christian women who gather to exorcise Beloved.

36. *Bluest Eye*, 108.

constructive black theology. So to fulfill God's plan of liberation for the African American church and community, a black theology today does well to hear the "unorthodox" (and seemingly threatening) voices and seek out life giving syncretistic practitioners of divine spiritual healing and saving.

Embodiment in Her Immediate Community

The tradition of a mother's relation to her daughter in Morrison's novels reveals the essence of embodiment in a poor black woman's immediate community. Women share a particular connection to their female children through nurturing from sickness to health, offering protection, passing on knowledge, and providing the nutrients of life. Claudia (in *The Bluest Eye*) has fond memories of her childhood autumns due to the doctoring role of her mother. Unable to hire a professional doctor who would charge money for his services, Claudia's mother repeatedly sat at her bedside during bouts of illness. The hands of motherhood literally nurture the illness out of Claudia's weak body. She thinks about the healing hands of her mother during the late hours of the evening: "when my coughing was dry and tough, feet padded into the room, hands repinned the flannel, readjusted the quilt, and rested a moment on my forehead." The closeness of the mother–daughter spiritual touch during sickness sketched such a graphic and permanent picture on Claudia's consciousness that the coming and going of seasons now connected with the medicinal hands of her mother. "So when I think of Autumn," resumes Claudia, "I think of somebody with hands who does not want me to die."[37] For Claudia, then, a mother's powerful hands literally resurrect and deliver her from death's door.

Moreover, mothers do not only fight off the threat of deadly diseases from their little girls. Especially when men attack their daughters, mothers also draw on hidden reserves of spiritual strength and risk potential bodily harm to themselves. Such a "foolishness" of a mama's protectiveness motivates Pilate to draw a knife on a man who has wrongfully slapped her daughter. Slowly Pilate approaches the male aggressor from behind, whips her arm around the man's throat, presses a knife against his heart, and waits for him to feel the knife blade. The man checks the rhythm of his breathing for fear he might cause the steel to sink in. Now with the might of the man neutralized by the touch of near death, Pilate calmly informs him about the spiritual bond between mother and daughter. "Women are foolish, you know, and mamas are the most foolish of all . . . First real misery I ever had in my life was when I found out somebody—a teeny tiny boy it was—didn't

---

37. Ibid., 14.

like my little girl."[38] If the initial real pain and misery suffered by Pilate in her life merely came from a little schoolboy not liking her daughter, then her spiritual whirlwind to protect her now adult daughter could possibly drive her to unknown acts of "foolishness." Hearing quite clearly Pilate's words, the former male attacker runs down the road when released from her grip.

Similarly, black mothers pass on vital knowledge to their daughters, important information such as how to be a woman. Mothers train their daughters to survive in a hostile world bombarded with demonic spirits of racial oppression, gender discrimination, and poverty exploitation. In order to make it to womanhood, therefore, daughters have to possess a wisdom of survival that helps them continue their lives and reach their goal of freedom—both the free ability to name their own nature (the cultural self) and to move about based on their own decisions (the political self).

To this end, Jadine receives the following counsel from her surrogate mother, Ondine, in *Tar Baby*. "Jadine, a girl has got to be a daughter first . . . And if she never learns how to be a daughter, she can't never learn how to be a woman." In the very mix of the mother–daughter ties flow information, tradition, strategy, perspective and the particular instruction that transforms a daughter into a woman. But this wisdom of womaness appears only when the daughter cares about her maternal roots. Accordingly, accountability comes with the acceptance of the answers of womanhood given to daughter from mother. Continuing her maternal role, Ondine states, "A daughter is a woman who cares about where she come from and takes care of them that took care of her."[39] The female child blossoms into an image of her mother because the daughter's spirituality (e.g., her political and cultural being as a woman) increases in proportion to her acceptance of her ties to her mother.

In addition, mothers defy the clutches of death so they can provide the nutrients of life for their daughters. For example, Sethe, without assistance, escapes from the lethal snares of slavery only to find herself on the edge of dying before she can cross the Ohio River to liberation. She experiences swollen, numb legs and bloody whip wounds drenching her back, while calling on the spiritual strength from within to carry her nutrients of life to her baby daughter. "All I knew was I had to get my milk to my baby girl," exclaims Sethe. The drive to give milk, the only life sustenance for her daughter, empowers her and focuses her mission with a singleness of mind. No thing, not even the boundaries of death, or nobody could have captured her. Because she knew only one reality—the possession of liquid life for the

---

38. *Song of Solomon*, 94.
39. *Tar Baby*, 281.

survival of her female baby's physical life—Sethe passionately concludes: "Nobody knew that but me and nobody had her milk but me."[40]

Finally, in certain cases, harmful circumstances force little black daughters to assume the role of mother when a negative spirituality slowly sucks the living spirit for survival and wholeness out of their mothers. The evil intent of the returned she-devil, Beloved, does exactly this. "Beloved ate up [Sethe's] life." She sat around and ate up every piece of food in the house, while her mother starved herself in submission to the she-devil spirit. Sethe, the mother, began to resemble a "teething child." Even after the black women of the community exorcise Beloved from their neighborhood, Sethe still suffers from physical and mental weaknesses. Therefore to protect her mother against the effects of the devilish thing, Sethe's other daughter, Denver, takes on two jobs.[41] In situations of crisis, the mother–daughter relationship can produce role reversals whereby a mother's childlike state forces a daughter to become substitute mother. Nevertheless, the substance of the tradition of embodiment in her immediate community, expressed with the mother–daughter connection, remains the same despite role exchange.

Embodiment in Her "Broader Community" and in the "Natural Body"

African American women's spirituality presents at least two more traditions of embodiment for black theological development: (1) the broader community and (2) the natural body. First, we look at the powerful imagery of Africa, representing poor black women's broader community.

Removed from the distant shores of Africa, poor black women still have a special tradition of ties to Africa, the mother continent. The power of Pilate (e.g., her conjuring abilities, clarity as a woman and as a mother, love for the folk, veneration of black ancestors, courage to move about, and more) comes from her being the link between those living in her family and their origins in Africa. Besides her strong female-spirituality qualities suggesting an African beginning, her very physical features confirm that African tradition planted, incubated, nurtured, and birth all her wisdom. Confirming this certainty, Macon Dead the elder tells his son, "If you ever have a doubt we from Africa, look at Pilate." She lives in testimony to Africa. Somehow the tradition from Africa to African America comes by way of a female connection. Not that black men play no small part passing on

40. *Beloved*, 16.

41. Ibid., 266. The description of Sethe's slow demise to an infantile state is fond on p. 250.

cultural values from the mother continent. Rather, black women's spirituality spreads with a gripping sense of who they are and where they come from. With such powerful clarity about their ties to the broader African diaspora, women's spiritual experience gives life to the entire black environment.

As a child, Sethe likewise receives knowledge of her own link to Africa. Nan, who cared for her since white men hung her biological mother, explains how she and Sethe's mother "were together from the sea." Both her mother and Nan spoke an African language that Sethe understood in her early childhood days. But since Nan's death and slavery's burdens, she has forgotten the specificities, sounds, and syntax. Yet, what remains in Sethe's consciousness was "the message—that was and had been there all along." The historical consciousness that poor black women have regarding their African relationship is not a mere infatuation with things long dead. Rather, Africa, with its forgotten language, provides significance for today. Specifically, the exact memory of origins still suggests to the descendants of memory that they have a place of beginnings created not by their contemporary oppressive constraints but by divinity. Therefore a free place of origin implies a historical moment in which both self-identity and self-determination existed as the standard. And so, knowledge of a fighting and survivalist spirit from Africa, the message, becomes a tradition passed from one female generation to another.

In fact, the resurrection of the African consciousness in all its coded and shadowy meanings comes to Sethe when she passes on to her daughter, Denver, the story of her hanged mother. No doubt Denver too will link her own future daughter into the tradition web of intergenerational bonds to Africa, and the cycle of story-Africa-woman-to-woman tradition continues. Black theology needs to look into sources of liberation found in a spiritual tie to Africa. And the intergenerational tradition that poor black women have with Africa presents one important place to discover the liberating spirit from that continent.

Another dark-skinned, tar-baby-looking woman shows the strong African tradition of poor black women. We find her in a Parisian grocery store where her sheer striking African presence disrupts the normal activity of this food establishment. Her skin like tar contrasted with her dazzling canary dress. Wearing many-colored sandals and sporting family markings engraved in her cheeks and a gelee wrapped around her hair, this African reveals a positive femaleness. She is a "woman's woman" and a "mother/sister/she," filled with "unphotographable beauty."[42] In fact, her beingness is summoned up in the word "she." She owns womanist traditions (e.g., she

---

42. *Tar Baby*, 45, 46, and 48.

connects with herself, her immediate and broader communities), and because color and body qualities help to define her, she embraces nature. In a word, she is extremely clear on her identity, and she moves about Paris, indeed the world, with grace, ease, and self-determination.

This African character opens up a treasure of spiritual self-determination and self-identity. Drawing on her own spiritual self-sufficiency, she teaches a black theology that its African spirituality helps black theology to reconnect to the depths of its foundational identity. The African tradition and survival in North America points to a createdness by God, "in the beginning." And black theology's acknowledgment of God's first creation of African Americans serves as acceptance of self-identity. At stake stands the question of whether or not the European Christian slave trade invented black Americans when they were brought as slaves to Jamestown, Virginia, in August 1619, or whether the divine created them in the many west coast African empires prior to the European Christian merchants' arrival to hunt for black skins. Who has creation power—God or the structures of white Christian commerce?

Self-identity then creates an awareness of all things being possible when one accepts God's power in creation—even the possibility of black people reclaiming the space around them. So accepting a persisting African spirituality, particularly the symbolic mediating role of this presence found in the abovementioned African woman in Paris, can provide courage and vocational focus to stay the course for both cultural (i.e., self-identity) and political (i.e., self-determination) liberation. The birth and legacy of black people exist in a sacred place before America, a location of time and a place of being free from systemic assaults on their looks and thought. If African Americans have in fact a prior new beginning before the present, they can have courage that a sacred beginning defeats any present-day attacks on their African family background. Consequently, the sacred beginning affirms that background and provides a current sense of pride in being someone with meaning and purpose in this world on earth.

Unfortunately, Jadine, the major black female character in *Tar Baby* (who flees in fear from some black swamp women), attempts to escape from this African woman in Paris and thereby to break a lifeblood connection to her extended community. The mere presence of the tar-baby beauty runs Jadine out of Paris. Furthermore, Jadine feels derailed; she feels lonely and "inauthentic." Her lonesome emotion comes from deserting Africa and the broader community. Her derailed depression comes from a lack of self-conscious personality.

More specifically, Jadine had grown up in a poor, working-class family in Baltimore. But a white male capitalist patron turned her into a white-black middle-income woman. Jadine's profound schizophrenic racial identity can only achieve a healthy resolution when she feels authentic. Yet her authenticity will appear only after and when she names and claims her tradition of embodiment in Africa; for the fountainhead of African American female spirituality is Africa.[43]

Finally, black women's embodiment in their natural bodies concludes this overall section on traditions of embodiment in women's spirituality. Poor African American women accept the natural state of their bodies as a sacred temple of self-love, normal physical-emotional expression, and a gift to God's spirit in worship. Particularly, Baby Suggs (in *Beloved*) pastors a congregation of poor black folk out in a section of the woods they call the Clearing. Here this unchurched preacher woman teaches her "church" to love the flesh of their bodies and to give full play to their natural appetites for crying, laughter, and dance. Put differently, this Christian conjurer calls on her people to lift up their spirits, through their bodies in liturgy and supplication, to divine spirit.

First, church service begins with Baby Suggs's sermon on self-love of their sacred flesh. "Here," preaches Baby Suggs, "in this here place, we flesh; flesh that weeps, laughs; flesh that dances on bare feet in grass. Love it. Love it hard." Why does she stress the specific passion of love of the body in her sermon? Suggs speaks within a concrete and historical context of white racism, a context quite familiar to her congregation's memory and to their daily and dehumanizing relations to the whites' slave system. Continuing her spiritual sharing of the body's importance, she reminds her folk that "they" (i.e., referencing white political and cultural standards) despise poor blacks' "eyes" and "the skin on your backs"; "they" do not love black hands; and "they ain't in love with your mouth." Instead, her congregation must love their flesh; stroke their hands and touch other black folk with them; grace their necks; support their backs; provide strong arms for their shoulders; and love their inside parts. Above all, climaxes Baby Suggs's speaking truth, "hear me now, love your heart. For this is the prize."

The heart beats as the ultimate part of the body because God has given poor blacks the ability to love each other, nonblacks and themselves. But in order to be human—to take God's grace of love, planted spiritually within each heart, and love the rest of humanity—black folk have to go down deep in the depths of their black hearts and love the blackness of their physical being. Self-love (i.e., coming to terms with the natural created love of God in human hearts) sets the context for having love of others, even feeling

---

43. In this section on embodiment in the broader community, see Pilate in *Song of Solomon*, 54; Sethe's talk with Denver, *Beloved*, 62; and the yellow dress African woman in *Tar Baby*, 45, 46, and 48.

compassion for one's enemies. Thus the natural bodies reflect sacred temples of self-love.

In her church services, moreover, Baby Suggs calls out the spirit through the normal physical-emotional expression of her congregation. With sacred authority, she calls the children and tells them to laugh before their parents. And the children's bodies, which they loved, filled the trees with laughter. She then orders the men to step forward and dance before their wives and children. And "groundlife shuddered under their feet" as the trees rang with the ongoing sounds of children's laughter. Finally, she calls the women and tells them to cry, for the living and the dead. It began with clear roles for each segment of the folk, but then everything and everybody intertwined and intermixed. "Women stopped crying and danced; men sat down and cried; children danced, women laughed, children cried until, exhausted and riven, all and each lay about the Clearing damp and gasping for breath. In the silence that followed, Baby Suggs, holy, offered up to them her great big heart."[44] In summary, Baby Suggs reveals through nature the spirituality of the individual and communal body in worship. Love of self, given by God's spirit of love and implanted in the heart, helps one's spiritual self-identity (i.e., a cultural claim), which, in turn, inspires one to fight off the "they's" of the world (i.e., a political claim), even to the point of compassion for the enemy. In addition, one shares God's spiritual love through open expressions of the body's natural activities of laughing, dancing, and crying. Therefore, Baby Suggs pulls together the necessity for black theology to develop a spirituality of the body. In worship, more exactly, poor black women's spirituality shares spiritual wisdom—the tradition of embodiment in poor black people's natural bodies.

Conclusion

In Toni Morrison's novels, poor black women's spirituality—an immortal, thus divine, spirit of liberation incarnated in poor African American women's traditions—teaches a constructive black liberation theology that God is a complete divinity whose power of liberation appears throughout the African American church and community. God's power of loving the poor through justice and freedom knows no boundaries. Consequently, a black liberation theology must open its heart and mind, ears and eyes to wider resources in the total African American spiritual experience. The novels of

---

44. See *Beloved*, 87–88, for a fuller treatment on Baby Suggs and the spirituality of the body.

Toni Morrison, then, provide one source for broadening our openness to God's spiritual involvement in human affairs.

Poor African American women's theological contributions to black theology prove that at least one vital role for poor black women's voice is sharing their experiences with God's free spirit. This spirit produces cultural and political expressions of vibrant traditions—thus an intergenerational process, a material and immaterial tradition of self-identity and self-determination, appear between grandmother, mother, and daughter. As a result, spirituality carries out definite acts, helping cultural claims of self-naming to empower oppressed individuals and communities to then subvert unjust social relations in order to control political places of liberation. Poor women's spirituality includes Christian and non-Christian thought and action. Such reflection-action does theology because it points to God's liberating spirit wherever God chooses to reveal God's Christian and non-Christian self.

Similarly, African American women's spirituality welcomes the religion of the institutional church and the nonchurch. It is religious because a powerful divine creativity among humanity expresses itself both within the church institution and, at the same time, within the broader African American women's community (which, of course, links to the rest of black folk and, in fact, to all of poor humanity). And so black theology has to open its eyes to see other institutional forms of black women's spirituality outside the recognized black-church structures.

If God brings freedom for all humanity, then this universal liberation will come from freeing poor African American women from class exploitation, racial oppression, and gender discrimination. Put differently, the more poor black women have the ability to define themselves and determine the space around themselves, the closer all humanity approaches the future new reality which God, through Jesus, offers to all. In this sense, black theology must take seriously the reality and possibilities of poor African American women serving a salvation role for the black church and community—indeed, for entire humanity.

God's liberation spirit reveals itself and incarnates itself within poor black women's traditions. Thus methodologically, one cannot begin with preconceived theological traditions (from above) and thereby restrict the multicolored garden of poor black women's religious experiences. Out of the soil of such spiritual realities a constructive black liberation theology will harvest new theological language, thought forms, metaphors, and categories.

In a word, women's spirituality teaches black theology the following: The more deeply black liberation theology accepts the richness of many voices of indigenous theological sources found within the African American church and community, the better chances are for constructing a complete black liberation theology movement that produces freedom not only for blacks but for all of suffering humanity. Poor African American women's experiences with the holy challenge black liberation theology to create a basic reorganization of interpersonal relations and to develop systemically a new social order.

Furthermore, to do theology from black women's literature is precisely theology. Why? Because the God of justice and love presented and discovered in African American religious traditions and contemporary practice is the same God who freely chooses to reveal an emancipatory spirit in black women's stories. Admittedly Christianity does not consistently serve as the explicit primary location for divine spiritual presence in Toni Morrison's novels. Still the liberating appearance of God's spirit in non-Christian revelations, through story, complements God's spiritual descending upon the decisive Christian revelation of Jesus the Christ ("The Spirit of the Lord is upon me"—Luke 4:18ff). God, as a result, provides a unique revelation in Jesus the Christ (for the Jesus follower) as well as a general revelation in all creation. In many cases, people syncretize their faith: when Christianity works, they use it; when parts of African religiosity functions well, they practice it; and when everyday folk wisdoms produce results, they make do with that.

Again, a fundamental theological and methodological issue is at stake here. Can poor African American women's traditions be authentic theological locations for divine freeing spirit? Black liberation theology must respond with a resounding yes! (Perhaps through laughing, dancing, crying, and loving its sacred body in the spirit.) Indeed, the originality of black women's spirituality experience and story must be taken seriously precisely because a black liberation theology receives and participates with an incarnational God who tabernacles with the poor. For black theology, one of the opportunities of the poor is the gender-racial-poverty challenge of African American women.

And while organizing the fight against wicked spiritualities, we also open ourselves up to the multiple positive, creative and spiritual laughter, tears, dance, and thinking of women. Womanist spirituality is a complete political and cultural Funk.

10

Working Together: Black and Womanist Theologies

I was a co-organizer of the first and only national dialogue between black liberation theology and womanist theology. That momentous and unique conference (indeed, the meticulous months of preparation, the intricate managing of participants during the course of the conference week, the postconference bubbles of further dialogue, and the book production of the presented papers) represented a process, not just an event, and showed a new mixing of thought and practice between male and female genders from the theory and ethics of African American perspectives. Consequently, *Walk Together Children: Black and Womanist Theologies, Church and Theological Education* (the resulting book of published papers from the historic black theology–womanist theology dialogue)[1] draws on the long religious, cultural, and singing history of blacks in the U.S.A. Through the slavery and emancipation days until now, black song has both nurtured and advanced African American life as a collective whole. Communality has always included a variety of individual experiences. Plurality and individuality have been part of the experimentation of what it meant to be black in the creation and development of North America. What has kept this tireless people in a corporate process is their walking together through good times and bad, relying on what W. E. B. Du Bois called their "dogged strength" to keep "from being torn asunder."[2] Somehow and someway they realized from historical memory or received from transcen-

---

1. *Walk Together Children* (Eugene, OR: Cascade Books, 2010); I am the lead editor.

2. W. E. B. Du Bois, *Souls of Black Folk*, Signet Classics (New York: New American Library, 1969), 45.

dental revelation that keeping on long enough on the road would produce ultimate fruit for the journey.

Indeed, the title of this black theology–womanist theology book plays off a singing classic gifted by African Americans to America and the world. "Walk Together Children. Don't You Get Weary. There's a Great Meeting in the Promised Land" is a line from one of the famous Negro Spirituals.³ The Negro Spirituals are songs created by and representative of the human effort of enslaved Africans and African Americans in North America, from 1619 to 1865.⁴ Physically chained, black bodies used song to create a "new world" identity out of a mixture of West African language groups.⁵ Differences merged into one people. Akan, Bakongo, Ndongo, Fante, Ibo, Woloof, Shona, Hausa, and Twi—some of the multiple West African language groups forced across the Atlantic in the white, European Christian slave trade—had to make common sense out of a common predicament.

What had happened to the diverse local ancestors of the families in each language group during the destabilizing process of enslavement? Were dead African ancestors upset because the living relatives had not performed

---

3. See John Lovell Jr., *Black Song: The Forge and the Flame; The Story of How the Afro-American Spiritual Was Hammered Out* (New York: Paragon, 1986), 278. Also William Francis Allen, et al., eds., *Slave Songs of the United States: The Classic Anthology* (1887; reprint, New York: Books for Library Press, 1971; and New York: Dover, 1995); Miles Mark Fisher, *Negro Slave Songs in the United States* (Secaucus, NJ: Citadel, 1978); R. Nathaniel Dett, ed. *Religious Folk-Songs of the Negro: As Sung at Hampton Institute* (Hampton, VA: Hampton Institute Press, 1927); James Weldon Johnson and J. Rosamond Johnson, *American Negro Spirituals: Two Volumes in One* (1925 and 1926; reprint, New York: Da Capo, 1977); James H. Cone, *Spirituals and the Blues* (1972; reprint, Maryknoll, NY: Orbis, 1991); and Shane White and Graham White, *The Sounds of Slavery: Discovering African American History through Songs, Sermons, and Speech* (Boston: Beacon, 2005).

4. Dwight N. Hopkins, *Down, Up & Over: Slave Religion and Black Theology* (Minneapolis: Fortress, 1999); Gayraud S. Wilmore, *Black Religion and Black Radicalism: An Interpretation of the Religious History of Afro-American People*, 2nd ed. (Maryknoll, NY: Orbis, 1983); Tim Hashaw, *Birth of Black America: The First African Americans and the Pursuit of Freedom at Jamestown* (New York: Carroll & Graff, 2007); Will Coleman, *Tribal Talk: Black Theology, Hermeneutics, and African/American Ways of "Telling the Story"* (University Park: Pennsylvania State University Press, 2000); and Albert J. Raboteau, *Slave Religion: The "Invisible Institution" in the Antebellum South* (New York: Oxford University Press, 1978).

5. John Russell Rickford and Russell John Rickford, *Spoken Soul: The Story of Black English* (New York: Wiley, 2000); J. L. Dillard, *Black English: Its History and Usage in the United States* (New York: Random House, 1972); Geneva Smitherman, *Talkin and Testifyin: The Language of Black America* (Detroit: Wayne State University Press, 1977); and Winifred Kellersberger Vass, *The Bantu Speaking Heritage of the United States* (Los Angeles: Center for Afro-American Studies, University of California Los Angeles, 1979).

correctly specific rituals? And what about the Almighty West African High God? Had this God abandoned ebony flesh squeezed between kneecaps and elbows on the Middle Passage slave ships from West Africa to North and South Americas and the Caribbean? And how did their identities fit into an empire of European modern nations around the Atlantic ocean?[6]

Yet many survived and sang/moaned across the watery journey from the ancient to the modern.

Thus the Negro Spirituals were singing testimonies of joyful people re-creating their collective self-identities out of traumatic time and space. These sacred songs united various language dialects into a black people, an African American people. Blacks or African Americans or African descendants in the Americas are created phenomena in recent human history.[7]

Moreover, not only did song develop a new corporate character. Negro Spirituals also show how a range of African-language speakers and singers converted and integrated white missionary Christianity on slave plantations (pre-1865) into a common West African view of the world and music rhythm. The practical daily life of an Africanized black people (that is, culture) already understood the world of spirits contained completely in the rituals of a total way of life. Restated, Negro Spirituals show us how enslaved black people's everyday spirituality took white missionary Christianity and re-viewed it through an African lens, and used it to make their sacred selves. These wailing and hopeful songs, ebony-performed sacred songs, plaintiff and defiant songs, are, indeed, the phenomenology of America and include a philosophy of history.

The Spirituals draw us into the raw reality and descriptive discussions about America's ancient origins. The recent creation of black people (recent in terms of human history) is the phenomenon upon which, to a

---

6. Robin Blackburn, *The Making of New World Slavery: From the Baroque to the Modern, 1492–1800* (New York: Verso, 1998); J. H. Elliott, *Empires of the Atlantic World: Britain and Spain in America, 1492–1830* (New Haven: Yale University Press, 2007); and Robin Blackburn, *The Overthrow of Colonial Slavery: 1776–1848* (London: Verso, 1990). I want to thank James A. Noel (professor at San Francisco Theological Seminary in San Anselmo, California) both for drawing my attention to these texts and for our lively and long conversations about what all of these means. On African endurance during this period and its meanings, see William St. Clair, *The Door of No Return: The History of Cape Coast Castle and the Atlantic Slave Trade* (New York: BlueRidge, 2007); Sylviane A. Diouf, *Dreams of Africa in Alabama: The Slave Ship* Clotilda *and the Story of the Last African Brought to America* (New York: Oxford University Press, 2007); and James T. Campbell, *Middle Passages: African American Journeys to Africa, 1787–2005* (New York: Penguin, 2006).

7. See Charles H. Long, "Perspectives for a Study of Afro-American Religion in the United States," in Long, *Significations: Signs, Symbols, and Images in the Interpretation of Religion* (Philadelphia: Fortress, 1986), 173–84.

large degree, the U.S. Constitution is formed. In that 1787 sacred document, blacks are referred to as three-fifths of a person, are by federal law obligated to be put back into slavery if they run away, and are given the 1808 date when they would be set free. The Constitution refers to black people at least three times. A large basis of the U.S. Constitution is slavery—the private property of a few white, wealthy men who founded the United States for their own family profit.

And when Negro Spirituals point to a big picture of historical deliverance of the enslaved, lyrics sing a speculative philosophy of history. When the Spirituals are suspicious of the possibility of slave masters logically and morally creating history, lyrics sound an analytic philosophy of history.

Simultaneously, the Spirituals contain an appreciation for syncretistic traditions of future time and space. In a sense, one could say that race, in its positive and negative expressions, is the foundation of knowledge, thus creating a contemporary (in the modern, 1492 "new world" context) way of knowing.[8]

Therefore, Spirituals sang of new phenomena (i.e., creations of African Americans and the nation of America), offered a critical philosophy of history, and talked about race as one basis of knowing reality.

Truly this process of adaptation, change, modification, unification, fragmentation, pragmatics, embedded worldview, and future hope define the Negro Spirituals. This erratic flow of new people–new religion is prominent in the words of the Negro Spirituals. "Walk Together Children"—even with your differences of language, shades of color, different genders and orientations, jobs, callings, vocations, unique gifts of the spirit, agreements and disagreements. It is a joyful and hopeful invitation to move forward together at this time and in this space. Walk now and not wait. Do it together and not alone. And be as children on two accounts.

Black Americans are literally the blood-children descendants of a whole bunch of West African forefathers and foremothers. As these children, remember to walk together now in historical memory of particular traditions good and bad. But also move forward without delay as spiritual children of God—made in God's image and possessing internally the vital force of divine breath. "Don't You Get Weary" separates getting physically tired from getting spiritually weary. Negro Spirituals allow for physical tiredness; even positive effort can test the body's endurance. But sacred song here gifts us with a calling of healed spirit and balanced life forces, which reduce

---

8. See M. C. Lemon, *Philosophy of History: A Guide for Students* (London: Routledge, 2003); Dermot Moran, *Introduction to Phenomenology* (London: Routledge, 2004); and Joseph Young and Jana Evans Braziel, eds., *Race and the Foundations of Knowledge* (Urbana: University of Illinois Press, 2006).

spiritual weariness. Healing and harmony repair, absorb, or overcome the weary and the worn out.

And if all the vibrant, joyful, pathological, wounded, and creative differences can just move now as children living in connection, striving for harmony and balance within the spirit and the external creation, there's a great meeting in the promised land. The "meeting" is us—the coming together of a "both-and" (rather than an "either-or") West African daily philosophy. The power of this spirit was and is its ability to absorb and use those who differ. And the newly created black selves and the newly created sacred selves used the life of Jesus, whose great big arms wrapped around all. This God came for everybody: the half and the whole, the good and the not so good, the churchgoer and those of other ritual practices.

In fact, this Jesus announced in Luke 4:16ff a road for all of the poor and their painful emotions. This Jesus concluded in Matt 25:31ff that denominations, Christianity, and individual beliefs do not matter to walk into heaven (i.e., the final great meeting in the promised land). The promised land is times and spaces where our individual and collective spiritual and societal harmony and balance grow faster than broken emotional selves and harmful social interactions with people and nature. The Negro Spiritual "Walk Together Children" teaches us something about going down this road.

And the essays in *Walk Together Children: Black and Womanist Theologies, Church and Theological Education* offer a window along this material-spiritual way. Contributors to this anthology hope to name, accept, and live with healthy tensions that prove creative catalysts for a complete and integrated life. Toward this end, people here represent the talking of women and men. Both together make sure that more resources and perspectives are brought to bear on routine and unexpected conditions of life. They both, united even with differences, present better a spirituality of connected walking. We harness powers and pain through recognizing the particularities of female and male genders that freely make a decision for comprehensive living and receive a transcendent something beyond solo walking. Moving in group increases and challenges the limited possibilities of only an individual worldview and faith.

Indeed, the idea of faith opens another pathway into these essays. For not only are men and women gathered here, but also we have two distinct yet connected bodies of knowledge sharing in conversation and criticisms over what it means to believe in something more than just what we can see. Black theology (i.e., knowledge created by black male religious self-reflection) and womanist theology (i.e., knowledge created by black female critical words and practice) have traveled into a destination of full scholarly disciplines; the former since the mid-1960s and the latter since the early 1980s.[9] Their status has become institutionalized in various movements and media within organizations of higher learning in the U.S.A. Black theology and womanist theology struggle to support each other in the American Academy of Religion, in the Society of Biblical Literature, in the Society for the Study of Black Religion, in courses within schools of theology, seminaries, divinity schools, and denominational colleges; at conferences and colloquia; in publishing, funding, generation grooming, internationalizing discussions, and in imagining dreams without drama.

And essays in this book are written by three leadership sectors of black and womanist theologies—professors, preachers, and the pew. Theology, broadly defined, means a renewed energy and commitment to be honest and reasonable on a journey of faith. It is critical and self-critical thinking about others' and an individual's fundamental ways of being in the world. At root, faith shows itself in at least two ways. First, how one spends one's time and manages one's feelings (from the moment one goes to sleep at night, through dreaming, to the details of actions performed in daylight, until bedtime returns) reveals the priorities of a faith. Second, if we had six months to live, what ways would we choose to walk? Data received in our dreams, intuitions, and daily details, connected to the inevitable time when we all die, will make final visions clear. In a word, we move beyond spiritual weariness towards clarifying our final life-and-death visions for ourselves and our children—in our great meeting in the promised land.

This clarification process of faith doing theology (that is, faith seeking understanding through intentionality) occurs at three levels, at least. Professors earn their living thinking critically about the academic discipline of theology all the time (i.e., systematic theology). Preachers receive a charge to shepherd a flock of people in daily full-time ministry (i.e., practical theology). And the pew practices the theory of faith talk in their theological wisdom outside of seminary lectures and preaching pulpits (i.e., folk theology). Still various contributors in this book walk in ambiguous ways in combinations of activist-preacher-pew person or preacher-theoretician or professor-hooper. Actually, hooping is the unique African American form of preaching that is singing.[10]

---

9. Diana L. Hayes, *And Still We Rise: An Introduction to Black Liberation Theology* (New York: Paulist, 1996); Stephanie Y. Mitchem, *Introducing Womanist Theology* (Maryknoll, NY: Orbis, 2002); Frederick L. Ware, *Methodologies of Black Theology* (Cleveland: Pilgrim, 2002); and Dwight N. Hopkins, *Introducing Black Theology of Liberation* (Maryknoll, NY: Orbis, 1999).

10. James Weldon Johnson, *God's Trombones: Seven Negro Sermons in Verse* (New York: Penguin, 1976); William H. Pipes, *Say Amen, Brother! Old-Time Negro Preaching*:

In addition to three types of black and womanst theologies, three generations of black and womanist scholars and practitioners have presented their voices. In that sense, *Walk Together Children* reveals the accumulated wisdom of the 1966 start of black theology and the 1980s origin of womanist theology. Intergenerational birthing of offspring and transmission of historical theory provides the heart of black and womanist theologies as disciplines. They are scholarly disciplines with archival importance bearing metaphors of meaning. And they are daily practices of spiritualized rituals in material routines. We here suggest integrating theoretical and practical aspects of disciplines. We sing our sacred songs and walk our roads together.

A key component of trilevel, intergenerational learning is the holding of hands among three biologically different age groups. In a word, essays are written by young adults (for instance, writers under thirty, with at least two younger than twenty-five when they wrote their chapters), middle-aged cohorts (for instance, those recognizing the unselfish power of their peer relations), and elder thinker-leaders (for instance, those who have already produced a legacy of texts and can see most clearly the historical future).

And then we meet varieties of blended contradictory and complementary positions throughout the book. Some writers are heterosexual, and others are self-identified lesbian and gay. Protestants and Roman Catholic authors contribute. Writers walk together from divinity schools, seminaries, schools of theology, religious studies departments, denominational colleges, and Christian education church sectors. Authors hold graduate degrees in many disciplines, including Bible, sociology of religion, systematic theology, ethics, interdisciplinary studies, cultural anthropology, musicology, education, pastoral and practical theologies, sociology, congregational ministry, systematic and contemporary studies, and environmental history.

Finally, the seven chapter headings describing the journey of conversations in *Walk Together Children* help women, men, the black church, and theological educators to walk together. Part 1 presents two sharp differences in black theology and womanist theology literature. Black theology's standard trademark stresses liberation, while a growing cadre of womanist theologians advocate survival and quality of life. James H. Cone's *Black Theology and Black Power* and *A Black Theology of Liberation* unapologetically centered, and thereby established as benchmark, liberation as the standard

---

A Study in American Frustration, African American Life Series (Detroit: Wayne State University Press, 1992); Henry H. Mitchell, *Black Preaching*, Harper's Ministers Paperback Series (New York: Harper & Row, 1979); Ella Pearson Mitchell, ed., *Those Preachin' Women* (Valley Forge, PA: Judson, 1985); Cleophus J. LaRue, *Heart of Black Preaching* (Louisville: Westminster John Knox, 2002); and Valentino Lassiter, *Martin Luther King in the African American Preaching Tradition* (Cleveland: Pilgrim, 2001).

of all authentic Christian identities in the U.S.A. While not dismissing liberation, Delores S. Williams's *Sisters in the Wilderness*[11] described survival and quality of life as more specific to African American women's realities. While the black man is out in the public square acting out his revolutionary agenda, black women have not only struggled but also had to provide practical survival strategies for a quality of life for themselves and the families' children. And, the truth be told, black women were doing survival and quality of life as well as being on the public front lines alongside African American men. So to create new moves with new angles, gender authorship is somewhat reversed around these two themes in Part 1 ("Liberation, Survival, and Quality of Life"). That is to say, two men speak on survival and quality of life—a usual womanist theme; and two women explore some aspects of liberation—a core black (male) theology concern. And the theme is divided between pastor and professor authors.

Part 2 ("Black Men and Patriarchy") connects directly two themes found both in higher education and in churches: the question of structures in society, higher education, and religious institutions allowing black men certain access while excluding African American women. Here too women take on a second related sub-topic (i.e., black men as endangered species), a topic mainly written about by African American men. Men writers confront squarely black male patriarchy, a theme discussed overwhelmingly by African American women. A good mixture of professor, pastor, and practitioner authors exists here as well.

Part 3 ("Jesus Man, Christ Woman") likewise reverses some themes. For instance, the core theme of this part specifically questions the standard church and professor's presentation of Jesus the Christ in an exclusive male-gender description. Here, this section recognizes the historical, biological Jesus as a man; women essayists touch on parts of this latter fact—that is, Jesus's maleness. Then "Christ as Woman" calls on men to examine Christ (i.e., the clear divinity status of Jesus) from a perspective of Christ's womaness. Indeed, if we are to journey in a fruitful way of renewal along the same path, then an important part of that walking dynamic and talking process is the willingness and practice of both conversational partners trying on the shoes (i.e., the perspective) of the other. That is what parts 1 through 3 achieve precisely. What does it mean to take each other's voices—research, writings, feelings, thinking, worldview—seriously? One way is to require

---

11. James H. Cone, *Black Theology and Black Power* (Maryknoll, NY: Orbis, 1969, reprinted, 2005); James H. Cone, *A Black Theology of Liberation*. Twentieth Anniversary Edition (Maryknoll, NY: Orbis, 1990; original ed., 1970); and Delores S. Williams, *Sisters in the Wilderness: The Challenge of Womanist God-Talk* (Maryknoll, NY: Orbis, 1993).

each partner to pick up the "walking stick" of the other and test out its intellectual beliefs in the hands of the person who did not originally create or carry the stick. In this way, both partners allow the spirit to use them to produce the amazingly new out of the initial apparently impossible. In other words, they all practice taking a crooked stick and hitting a straight lick.

Part 4 debates "Sexuality"—an obsessive and fanatical topic raging in North American society, churches, and schools. Two self-identified homosexual scholars (one gay and one lesbian) and two heterosexual scholars (one male and one female) take on this misunderstood, highly politically charged, and creative category of (both hetero- and homo-) sexual orientations. In this instance difference brings about clarity, learning, and partnership. At root, we are all human beings longing for daily experiences with the realities of nature and human interaction, and sensing our way through avenues of potentiality for ordinary and extraordinary meaning. Consequently, our success or our failure in helping someone else along the path judges all of us, regardless of who we love.

The final three sections speak to the future of women, men, the black church, and theological education. Part 5 ("The Future of Black and Womanist Theologies and the Church") goes directly into this overarching question. Part 6 ("New Voices in the Black Church") opens new avenues of health for and energizing of black and womanist theologies, including hip hop lifestyles and rap music, black environmental liberation theology, and young black men opting out of patriarchy and into allies for womanists by giving up male material power. Young people (without whom everything ends) and innovative, crackling thought (challenging outdated black and womanist theologies) fill this part.

The "Global Future," Part 7, claims fundamentally that if women and men, black theology and womanist theologies, professors and preachers, diverse sexual orientations, various professional generations, multiple age groups, and the black church and theological education are to survive, thrive, and, in certain instances, indicate a positive pathway for any to see, hear, and walk, then we all have to balance this process in a healing and healthy fashion. Black liberation theology and womanist theology both started in increasingly complex global relationships. Consequently, any serious reader of the foundational documents and of the complex contexts when both theologies were born will know both conversational partners have always, in various degrees, linked the domestic U.S. with international solidarity for the locked-out voices.

And so, dear readers, I point you in the direction of this book, *Walk Together Children: Black and Womanist Theologies, Church and Theological Education*, as a gift, as one possible model for how black liberation theology can participate in a refreshing and fruitful journey with womanist theology. Who knows? It might aid you in your own comings and goings along life's way.

Walk Together Children. Don't You Get Weary. There's a Great Meeting in the Promised Land.

www.ingramcontent.com/pod-product-compliance
Lightning Source LLC
Chambersburg PA
CBHW031434150426
43191CB00006B/509